Sempringham Studies

Eastern Europe 1918-1953

From Versailles to Cold War

Paul G. Lewis

Sempringham *publishing*, Bedford

Cover picture: A poster by Dmitry Moor showing a Soviet soldier stamping on Polish nationalism, 1920 (David King Collection, London).

Other illustrations: *Illustrated London News* pp. 19, 50, 64, 73, 84, 85 and 92; *Daily Express* p. 17; *Le Canard Enchaîné* p. 34; *Pravda* p. 51; *San Francisco Chronicle* p. 62; *Daily Worker* p. 65; *Star*, London p. 66; Punch Picture Library p. 70; *Chicago Sunday Tribune* p. 93; Sempringham Collection p. v.

The publisher will be glad to make suitable arrangements with any copyright holders whom it has not been possible to contact.

Sempringham Books are available (post free) to schools, colleges and individuals direct (10% discount on orders of 10 or more of the same title): Sempringham Books, PO Box 248, Bedford MK40 2SP.

Sempringham Books are distributed to booksellers by Central Books, 99 Wallis Road, London E9 5LN   Tel. 0181-986 4854.

ISBN 0 9515764 4 5

First published 1999

Impression number	10	9	8	7	6	5	4	3	2	1
Year			2004	2003	2002	2001	2000	1999		

Copyright © 1999 Paul G. Lewis

Designed and set by Sempringham publishing services, Bedford. Sempringham publishing, PO Box 248, Bedford MK40 2SP. Printed by Redwood Books, Trowbridge, Wiltshire.

Contents

To student readers and their tutors

Ways to use this book

The East European states, stretching from the Baltic to the Balkans, many created after the break up of the Austro-Hungarian and Russian empires as a consequence of the First World War and the peace treaties made afterwards, have in common their smaller size and weakness relative to the larger states to East and West. Their vulnerability to these stronger states is one reason for their importance and the drama of their histories in the first half of the twentieth century.

The number of states present a particular difficulty for the student and, indeed, writer of Eastern Europe. To help readers pick a path through the international aspects of the region and follow the histories of the individual states the chapters in this study are of two kinds. Chapters 1, 2 and 3 together with 7 and 8 provide the reader with the wider context and the issues for the Eastern European states between 1918 and 1953. Their purpose is to provide perspective and to help the reader make sure assessments and sound judgements. The core chapters, 4, 5 and 6, are longer and present the histories of these states. Before tackling the core chapters, students are advised to skim read the earlier and later chapters and note the key issues.

How a book is used will be dependent on students' study purpose. It is seldom the best procedure to read a textbook in a uniform way from beginning to end and with this text many students will wish to trace the History of only some of the Eastern European states. The core chapters, State Building and Problems of National Democracy in the 1920s (Chapter 4), Eastern Europe and the Resurgence of German Power in the 1930s (Chapter 5) and Stalin's Victory in Eastern Europe, 1943-1953 (Chapter 6), cover general issues at the beginning and end: in the middle the particular histories of the states are summarised. Readers will find it useful to read the 'Questions to consider' on the last page of the core chapters and then the general issues at the beginning and end (pages 42-55 in Chapter 4, pages 104-111 in Chapter 6), before individual histories are followed, by use of the subheadings which are repeated at the bottom of the page with running headings. The mixture of general issues' analysis and narrative in the core chapters enables student readers to make the assessments and judgements that advanced study requires. For further guidelines on how to use information to develop analysis and prepare essay answers consult Chapters 4, 6 and 7 of *The Good History Students' Handbook*, Edited by Gilbert Pleuger (Sempringham, 1993) or Chapters 3, 6 and 7 of *Undergraduate History Study - The Guide to Success* (Sempringham, 1997).

The two leaders whose policies played a large part in the histories of the smaller Eastern European states, during the 1930s-1950s, until their deaths

1 Overview and Issues

In contrast to the idea of a 'long nineteenth century' the twentieth century has come to be understood (on the suggestion of historian Eric Hobsbawm) as a short one, beginning in 1914 with the First World War and four devastating years of mechanised mass warfare and ending more optimistically in 1989 with the conclusion of the cold war and collapse of European communism. For Eastern Europe these are dates with particular significance. It was the First World War that broke the power of the decrepit multi-national empires and ushered in a modern Eastern Europe in 1918. And it was in Eastern Europe that communism first met its end in 1989 and opened up the prospect of a new era of pan-European democracy.

For Eastern Europe this 'short twentieth century' can be split into two halves. The first 35 years — from 1918 to 1953 — began with the establishment of a modern Eastern Europe composed of independent nation states on the West European model. They faced enormous challenges and experienced a precarious fate. The numerous small and medium-sized states first struggled to live up to the democratic principles that had attended their foundation and then had to cope with the growing strength of a Nazified Germany. There followed a further terrible war which waged throughout much of the region and the imposition of an alternative Russian tyranny masterminded by Joseph Stalin. The 36 years that followed — from 1953 to 1989 — fell into more of a single pattern. They were dominated by the search within a broad communist framework for a solution to the problems of a Russian-imposed Stalinism within Eastern Europe. It was increasingly a process that became identified with the running down of the communist dynamic as a whole as its economy continued to fall behind that of the West and people lost any residual faith in the communist ideal. It is the tumultuous events of the first half of this 'short century' in Eastern Europe with which this book is concerned.

The year 1918 was the date when Eastern Europe fully emerged in its modern form and assumed a distinctive identity within the Continent as a whole. Before the First World War broke out in 1914 much of the East of Europe formed part of several large, multi-national, generally long-established and often ramshackle empires. They numbered four — Austria-Hungary, Russia, Ottoman Turkey and (the youngest and most dynamic) Germany. Turkey's European empire had been retreating for some decades, and much of what remained was seized in the First Balkan War of 1912-13. In 1918 Turkey and Austria-Hungary were both defeated and their empires completely destroyed by the war. The end of empire within Europe was a general process. Russia and Germany were also beaten during the First World War — the former by the Central Powers and the latter by the Western Allies — and critically weakened, thus contributing to the emergence of an independent Eastern Europe. Russia and Germany, nevertheless, survived as major powers and came to exert an increasing influence over developments in the East of Europe.

The end of the First World War saw, therefore, the exhaustion of the power that had sustained the position of traditional empires for several centuries in that part of Europe. But it also involved the simultaneous weakening of two countries whose might was only temporarily disrupted and far from totally destroyed. Both Germany and Russia were showing considerable powers of recovery by the mid-1920s. It was an unprecedented and short-lived power vacuum in 1918 that inaugurated the period of Eastern Europe's modern independence in 1918. This was a situation that contained major elements of conflict and instability from the very beginning and presented the new states of Eastern Europe with major challenges from the moment of their birth (see page 16).

The maintenance of democracy and of independence within the new state framework proved to be extremely difficult. Democracy only really took root in Czechoslovakia, and by the end of the 1920s little remained of the democratic promise elsewhere in the region (Chapter 3). The Depression dealt a cruel blow to their weak economies, while the recovery of German power and — particularly — its capture by the Nazi movement of Adolf Hitler soon showed the weakness of the East Europeans' claim to national independence (Chapter 4). It took another world war, even more costly than the first, to smash the Nazi hold over the region — and this was achieved only by the gargantuan efforts of a revived Russia, whose primacy within Eastern Europe then left little scope either for democracy or for national independence (Chapter 5). But the hopes of 1918 were not all lost, as the wholly unexpected events of 1989 were eventually to show. The national forms of the East European countries and the different civilisations they represented were not buried or obliterated this time as fully as they had been with the rise of the former, longer lasting continental empires. They were only temporarily subdued and re-emerged when the power of Soviet Russia also weakened. After 1989 Eastern Europe was ready and again able to take up the twin causes of democracy and national independence.

Modern Eastern Europe thus emerged very much as a region wedged between major powers, of smaller nations located on the edge of territories inhabited by more powerful and numerous peoples. The territory of modern Eastern Europe can largely be defined as the space between Russia and Germany (and, to the south, Italy) — and has thus often been called the 'lands between'. It was, in the conception of Tomáš Masaryk (the founder of Czechoslovakia and its first president), a region of small nations and countries with a special interest in the preservation of a broader, peaceful European order. But while this gives a general idea of the nature of the region it does not necessarily provide a clear-cut definition of the countries included. The devastating expansion of German power in the 1930s and during the Second World War, as well as the unprecedented westward and southern extension of Soviet Russian power in the latter half of the war, suggests a particularly broad idea of the region during this period.

The history of Czechoslovakia, Hungary, Poland and the three Baltic states (Estonia, Latvia and Lithuania) were all very much dominated by the developing contest between Germany and Russia in the 1920s and 1930s — but then so were the Balkan countries of Romania, Bulgaria, Yugoslavia and Albania. Even Greece, although primarily a player in the Mediterranean region, suffered the common Balkan fate of German domination and remained (as Churchill's war-time negotiations with Stalin in October 1944 clearly showed; see page 90) one of the pawns in the broader great power game. While, at the other end of the north-south continuum, Finland lies on the edge of the Scandinavian world, it also ended up struggling against German as well as the historic Russian influence. Finally, mention is also made of Austria in this book. Although obviously a part of the German-speaking world it, too, became one of the smaller countries in 1918 with the collapse of the empire it had previously controlled, very much on the lines of Hungary. It also played a particular role in the rise of Nazism and the growing dominance of German power throughout the region.

The history of these countries between 1918 and 1953 raises issues that have a strong contemporary relevance. Several years after the event, the practical outcome of the beginning of the end of European communism in 1989 remains uncertain and its precise implications for the future of Europe unclear. One thing does stand out, though. Soon after the changes István Deák, a leading historian of Eastern Europe, stated clearly that the history of the inter-war period had to be thoroughly rethought and its implications for contemporary developments fully considered. The linking in this account of pre-Second World War history with the immediate post-war period encourages a more coherent view of East European developments throughout the twentieth century and contributes to a deeper understanding of its dynamics.

The experience of the inter-war period is relevant to several contemporary areas of uncertainty and potential instability. For one thing, the conflicts and problems of the pre-war period had by no means been wholly solved or completely marginalised by the intervening periods either of world war or of communist domination. Some of the major historical themes and challenges of the first half of the twentieth century have resurfaced with a surprising intensity towards its end. Movements of nationalism like that in

Serbia, popular anti-Semitism in Poland and anti-communism throughout the region pose new political problems. Questions of land reform and relative backwardness in terms of the economy have also re-emerged in the Eastern Europe of the 1990s and provide new challenges for contemporary political leaders. In the area of international relations there are new problems surrounding a further resurgence of German power and relations with a weakened and often resentful Russian neighbour, as well as others concerning the appropriate place of the region in a recast Europe. These issues that dogged the pre-war politics of the region have now returned to haunt the political landscape at the end of the century. The way in which these problems moved on to the political agenda and the manner in which they were tackled after the First World War carry significant lessons for the future. They are issues that lie at the heart of the story told in this book.

Chronological table

1918

14 October	Czechoslovak national council declares independence.
17 October	Hungarian parliament declares independence from Austria.
3 November	Independent Polish Republic proclaimed.
1 December	The kingdom of Serbs, Croats and Slovenes is declared.

1919

17 January	Communist government takes power in Hungary.
28 June	Peace Treaty of Versailles signed.
1 August	Romanian troops occupy Budapest; communist government falls.
17 August	Overwhelming victory of Peasant Party in Bulgarian elections.

1920

18 April	Elections in Czechoslovakia produce coalition government.
25 April	Polish-Soviet war breaks out; ends in October with Polish victory.
4 June	Treaty of Trianon signed; major Hungarian territorial losses.
14 August	Czechoslovakia signs treaty with Yugoslavia.

1921

3 March	With Soviet Russia weakened, Romania annexes Bessarabia.
20 March	Silesia partitioned between Poland and Germany by League of Nations.
14 April	Hungarian stabilisation begins under Count Bethlen.

1922

8 January	Plebiscite of local population transfers town of Vilnius, formerly belonging to Lithuania, to Poland.
16 April	Rapallo Treaty signed by Germany and the Soviet Union.
11 October	Formal end of Greek/Turkish war with massive defeat for Greece.
30 October	Italian Fascists form government in Rome.

1923

9 January	French and Belgian troops occupy the Ruhr valley in Germany.
9 June	Stamboliiski overthrown in Bulgaria and subsequently murdered.

1924

25 January	Defence and aid treaty signed by Czechoslovakia and France.
16 August	Acceptance of Dawes Plan reducing German reparations.
28 December	Abdication of Carol's claim to Romanian Crown; goes into exile.

1925

21 January	Albania proclaimed republic.
4 May	Communists outlawed in Bulgaria after mass bombing.
16 October	Locarno Conference attempts to secure European peace.

1926

12 May	Rebellion against Polish government led by General Piłsudski.
8 September	Germany admitted to League of Nations.

1929

5 January	King Alexander proclaims dictatorship in Yugoslavia.
28 October	Wall Street Crash; largest one-day drop in share prices.

1931

20 March	German/Austrian customs union; France recalls loans.
11 May	Failure of *Creditanstalt* in Austria, largest East European bank.

1932

9 July	End of Lausanne conference and of payment of German reparations.
17 July	Electoral victory of Peasant Party in Romania.

1933

31 January	Hitler appointed German Chancellor.
17 June	Hungarian prime minister Gömbös visits Hitler.

1934

25 July	Chancellor Dollfuss assassinated by Austrian Nazis.
18 September	Soviet Union joins League of Nations.
9 October	Yugoslav King Alexander assassinated in Marseilles.

1935

16 March	Hitler renounces disarmament clauses of Versailles Treaty.
13 December	Beneš succeeds Masaryk as Czechoslovak president.

1936

7 March	German army occupies Rhineland in breach of Locarno Treaty.
11 May	Trade agreement between Germany and Yugoslavia.
15 October	Establishment of German-Italian Axis.

1937

16 October	Formation of 'Arrow Cross' by Hungarian National Socialists.
28 December	New Romanian government introduces anti-Jewish laws.

1938

10 February	King Carol pronounces dictatorship in Romania
10 March	Austrian *Anschluss*, union of the German-speaking countries.
29-30 September	Munich conference accedes to Hitler's Sudetenland demands.

1939

16 March	Bohemia and Moravia proclaimed German protectorates.
31 March	Military commitment of Britain and France to help Poland in case of attack.
7 April	Italy invades Albania.
23 August	Non-aggression pact between Germany and Soviet Union.
1 September	German invasion of Poland.
3 September	Britain and France declare war on Germany.
17 September	Soviet invasion of Eastern Poland as agreed with Germany.
30 November	Soviet Union invades Finland, expelled from League of Nations.

1940

10 May	Beginning of German Western offensive.
15 June	Soviet army occupies Baltic Republics.
22 June	French armistice with Germany.
7 October	German troops enter Romania.
20 November	Hungary joins Axis.

1941

6 April	Germany attacks Yugoslavia to secure access to Greece.
22 June	Germany attacks the Soviet Union.
25 November	Bulgaria joins Axis.
4 December	German attack on Moscow halted.
7 December	Japanese attack on United States naval base at Pearl Harbour brings America into war.
11 December	Declaration of war on United States by Germany and Italy.

1942

20 January	Wannsee Conference confirms plans for extermination of Jews.
8 May	German summer offensive in southern Russia begins.

1943

31 January	German sixth army contingent surrenders at Stalingrad.
5 May	Indefinite adjournment of Hungarian parliament.
25 July	Overthrow of Mussolini; Italy surrenders in September.
28 November	Meeting in Teheran of Churchill, Roosevelt and Stalin.

1944

19 March	German occupation of Hungary begins.
1 August	Warsaw Uprising breaks out.
15 August	Coup by King Michael and declaration of Romanian surrender.
31 August	Bucharest occupied by Red Army.
5 September	Bulgaria requests armistice with Soviet Union.

1945

17 January	Soviet troops take Warsaw.
4 February	Beginning of Yalta conference.
6 March	New government under communist influence in Romania.
8 March	Tito establishes new Yugoslav government.
11 April	Entry of Red Army into Vienna.
2 May	Occupation of Berlin by Red Army.
8 May	End of war in Europe.
28 June	Provisional government in Poland dominated by Soviet protégés.
17 July	Opening of Potsdam conference in Germany.
4 November	National elections in Hungary.
11 November	Elections in Yugoslavia produce massive communist majority.
18 November	Victory of Bulgarian National Front not recognised by US.

1946

11 January	Albania declared first People's Republic in Eastern Europe.
5 March	Churchill's 'Iron Curtain' speech in Fulton, Missouri.
26 May	Communists get 38 per cent of vote in Czechoslovak elections.
27 October	Communists win elections after coercive campaign in Bulgaria.
9 November	Communist victory in Romania following mass intimidation.

1947

5 January	Hungarian opposition deputies accused of conspiracy.
19 January	Communist victory in Poland in further rigged election.
5 June	Proclamation of Marshall Plan for European economic recovery.
6 August	Show trial of Bulgarian opposition leader Petkov (later hanged).
31 August	Victory of communist-dominated National Front in Hungary.
22 September	Establishment of Cominform to reinforce Soviet domination.
12 November	Romanian opposition leader sentenced to life imprisonment.

1948

25 February	Communist-dominated government in Czechoslovakia.
12 June	Hungarian social democrats merged with communist party.
27 June	Czechoslovak social democrats merged with communist party.
28 June	Yugoslavia expelled from Cominform.

1949

25 January	Comecon founded to further integration of communist economies.
24 September	Show trial of Rajk and associates ends in Hungary.
7 October	Proclamation of (communist) German Democratic Republic.
7 December	Show trial of Kostov in Bulgaria ends with death sentence.

1950

23 May	Communists win 98 per cent of vote in Albanian elections.
25 June	Beginning of Korean War.
6 July	East Germany recognises Oder-Neisse border with Poland.

1951

1 May	US-funded Radio Free Europe starts broadcasts to Eastern Europe.
July	Hungarian interim primate Grősz sentenced to fifteen years in prison.
September	Reintroduction of rationing in Poland.

1952

February	Further nationalisation measures introduced in Hungary.
20 November	Opening of trial in Czechoslovakia of Slánský and associates.
22 November	Promulgation of new constitution in Poland.

1953

5 March	Death in Soviet Union of Joseph Stalin.

2 The Social and Economic Context

The historical legacy

Eastern Europe was not created out of a void in 1918. Some of its countries might have been newly established but the region had a rich historical legacy. The lands to the East had been the site of major dynasties and empires, the birthplace of civilisations and site of important social, cultural and political accomplishments from the early stages of the Continent's history. Various kingdoms and early forms of empire had existed in the area from the Middle Ages, ranging from Serbia and Bulgaria in the south to Hungary, Bohemia and Poland farther north. The northern countries in particular formed part of the increasingly complex network of political and cultural relations throughout the Continent as a whole. In this, however, they were not so much 'Eastern' as simply part of the developing culture of Europe as a whole. Like the West of the Continent, too, Eastern Europe received many migrant populations and contained diverse ethnic mixtures throughout its varied territory. This tended to continue longer in the East as the ethnic makeup of the West became more stable. The area saw several major movements of peoples and the arrival of various conquering tribes and dynasties — from East to West during the first millennium (Slavs and Huns), followed later by the gradual eastward infiltration of German settlers from the time of the Middle Ages as well as the arrival of stateless groups like Jews and gypsies. Pressures from the East were maintained with the continuing expansion of the Ottoman empire and the growing power of Russia.

Unlike Western Europe, though, the East did not experience the development of strong modern monarchies or the rise of powerful states like England, France or — eventually — the unified Germany. This was to be a major condition of the relative decline of the region in the nineteenth century. Some countries which had been quite powerful within Eastern Europe during the seventeenth and eighteenth centuries lost their position as the West entered a phase of modernisation and rapid development. Politically, economically and militarily the eastern part of Europe declined in relation to the West as the modern period began and a new form of society came into being. Eastern Europe was increasingly caught between the rising powers of the West and growing pressures from the East, and the geopolitical position of the region became correspondingly critical.

Over the centuries the Ottoman Turks had advanced slowly but irresistibly from the south-east into the heart of east-central Europe. After the fall of Byzantium they conquered the Balkans and were only halted in 1693 outside Vienna by a powerful army led by the Polish king, Jan Sobieski. The region had also faced the inexorable rise of Russia from its origins in the principality of Moscow to the development of a major power which was able to absorb great areas of the former Polish-Lithuanian Commonwealth. The final extinction of Polish independence in 1794 meant the end of the old historic East European states and the full consolidation of the rule of the great imperial powers in the north of the region. But even as Poland disappeared from the map with the final partition of its territory between Russia, Prussia and Austria there were clear signs that the crumbling of the Ottoman empire was under way in the south. In 1817 a version of an independent Serbian state had already come into existence, while Greece also stood on the verge of national independence. Related national movements also brought greater autonomy to parts of modern Romania and, eventually, Bulgaria. After the First Balkan War of 1912-13 little remained of Turkey's European empire, although the three other empires continued to dominate the rest of the region (see map, page 12).

The modern invention of Eastern Europe

Signs of the modern Eastern Europe thus began to emerge before its new territories took a clear shape or its distinctive political identity was formed in the early twentieth century. Much of this outcome was to depend on broader European developments and the pattern of events that unfolded in the West. But the course of history is strongly influenced by ideas as much as it is the concrete outcome of a particular balance of political and military power. The very idea of Eastern Europe in the twentieth century was strongly influenced by new cultural and intellectual perspectives that arose in the dynamic societies of Western Europe. Conceptions of Europe itself had been subject to radical transformation. In classical times the area of Mediterranean civilisation had generally been distinguished from the barbarian north, and this lateral division of an increasingly complex Europe which reflected on its own identity lasted through the Renaissance into the early modern period. It was only in the eighteenth century under the influence of writers of the Enlightenment, it has recently been argued, that the critical division of Europe came to be seen as one running from north to south. Within this framework a particular kind of Eastern Europe came to be 'invented' — one that was characterised by overall backwardness and generally lacked the attributes of civilisation. It was a region that was emphatically different from the West of the Continent; in this Eastern Europe people's habits were different and an alien language (generally Slavonic in character) was spoken.

Eastern Europe, 1914

0   250
km

– – – Line dividing the Hungarian
Kingdom from the remainder
of the Habsburg Empire

SWEDEN

DENMARK

Copenhagen   *Baltic Sea*

RUSSIAN EMPIRE

Danzig   Königsberg

River Vistula

Berlin   Warsaw

River Bug

GERMAN EMPIRE

Lemberg
(Lvov)

GALICIA   BUKOVINA

River Dniester

AUTRO-HUNGARIAN
EMPIRE

River Danube   *Carpathians*   *River Pruth*

Munich   Vienna

Budapest   TRANSYLVANIA

SWITZ

Carpathians

CROATIA

Agram
(Zagreb)   BANAT   ROMANIA

DOBRUDJA

BOSNIA-
HERCEGOVINA   Belgrade   Bucharest

Dinaric Alps

DALMATIA

ITALY

Adriatic Sea

SERBIA   BULGARIA

Sofia

MONTENEGRO   MACE-
DONIA   Constantinople

Rome

Tirana   ALBANIA   THRACE   OTTOMAN
EMPIRE

GREECE

Document: Count Ségur, minister and envoy of Louis XVI, on his journey to St Petersburg in 1784.

In traversing the eastern part of the estates of the king of Prussia, it seems that one leaves the theatre where there reigns nature embellished by the efforts of art and a perfected civilisation. The eye is already saddened by arid sands, by vast forests. But when one enters Poland, one believes one has left Europe entirely, and the gaze is struck by a new spectacle: an immense country almost totally covered with fir trees always green but always sad, interrupted at long intervals by some cultivated plains, like islands scattered on the ocean; a poor population, enslaved; dirty villages; cottages little different from savage huts; everything makes one think one has been moved back ten centuries, and that one finds oneself amid hordes of Huns, Scythians, Veneti, Slavs, and Sarmatians.

Larry Wolff, *Inventing Eastern Europe: the Map of Civilisation on the Mind of the Enlightenment* (1994).

The importance of this view lies not in its accuracy or fictional character (a large part of the picture was indeed mythic) so much as in the identification of a separate and distinctive Eastern Europe. Just as important was the fact that this identity was formed on the basis of a western view of European civilisation and was marked by experience of its characteristic path of development. Such views gained strength as the West of the Continent began to outstrip the East more noticeably in terms of political and economic development, and sharper divisions in terms of economic growth and diverse forms of social modernisation became apparent. Modern western conceptions were equally influential in underpinning the creation of a twentieth-century Eastern Europe after the First World War (see Chapter 3). This was defined essentially in terms of the nation-state and was designed to be governed according to the principles of parliamentary democracy. It might, indeed, be argued that this train of thought runs straight through to the 1990s to emerge as a driving force in the post-communist reformation of the area following blueprints of market capitalism and liberal democracy.

East European backwardness

The primary characteristic of the Eastern Europe that dominated early western conceptions of the region was that of its overall backwardness, or a relatively undifferentiated 'barbarism' as the self-proclaimed civilised westerners of the eighteenth century had termed it. But the social and cultural complexity of the region became clearer with the dissolution of the old empires. It contained people of different faiths, various races and divergent ethnic origin — many of them living in close proximity within the borders of the same country. The Eastern Europe that appeared in 1918 was marked by numerous internal divisions in terms of ethnicity, religion and historical inheritance.

Urbanisation, industrial revolution and the march of progress further marked the emergence of modern Eastern Europe. Long-established divisions were overlaid and tensions often exacerbated by the diverse pressures of modernisation, involving such processes as economic development, industrialisation, the growth of towns, the spread of education, influences associated with regional and international trade patterns, and — by no means the least important factor — the rapid growth of population. Nevertheless, framing the political and ethnic mosaic that emerged after 1918 were overall social and economic uniformities that distinguished Eastern Europe from the West of the Continent and the greater progress made there in terms of economic and industrial development.

The Eastern Europe invented by western intellectuals in the eighteenth century was undoubtedly a socially and economically backward one, as well as being distinguished by strong cultural and linguistic differences which were often its most striking feature to the western observer. The predominance of people speaking a different language, generally Slavonic rather than German, was one of the clearest signs of Eastern Europe's difference. But other kinds of division were just as important and exercised a more profound influence on the ways in which the region developed during the nineteenth and twentieth centuries. Eastern Europe was, certainly in terms of population numbers, primarily a peasant society. It lay to the East of what is often described as one of the most fundamental frontier lines that traversed Europe and its history, that which divided the areas in which serfdom disappeared in the fifteenth and sixteenth centuries from those where the subjection of the farming population to a ruling caste lasted until the nineteenth. It was not just that they were poor and generally lived a life of abject misery. Agricultural workers were not slaves, but many of them had limited rights of movement and property and were not fully free citizens. Serfdom was abolished only in 1848 in Austria-Hungary, in Prussia in the 1850s and in Russia in 1861.

The late survival of serfdom meant that agriculturists were subject to the legal and economic power of gentry and aristocratic groups and did not enjoy the formal independence of their western counterparts — although in practice legal freedom had often actually resulted in the impoverishment of western peasantries and their expulsion from the land as farmers and larger estate-owners developed more intensive forms of agriculture that was more efficiently organised and made more use of machinery. But there was growing social mobility and movement from country to town, as well as strengthening links between agriculture and the growing industrial sector. The West thus experienced both a 'push' and 'pull' effect in this respect in terms of industrial development, movement out of rural areas and the growth of towns which was largely absent in the East. Different parts of Eastern Europe varied in this respect, and much often depended on which imperial power dominated. In the areas ruled by Turkey the situation in the countryside was quite diverse in terms of peasant property. Less land was transferred to peasants in Romania, while in Serbia and Bulgaria the former large land-holdings were mostly broken up. The general effect, however, was to leave a large proportion of the population dependent on relatively unproductive land resources and to reproduce a social structure more traditional and less favourable to economic — and particularly industrial — development than in the West.

Social structure, culture and national differences

Rural conditions made it very difficult for the new states of Eastern Europe to deal with the economic situation that confronted them after 1918 and to create a framework for effective national development within the frontiers of the new states (and, eventually, to cope with the effects of the world-wide Depression that emerged at the end of the 1920s). Problems of social and economic development were further enhanced by contrasting social inheritances and the way in which ruling groups in different nations like Hungary, Poland and the Croatian part of Yugoslavia had tended to retain much of their aristocratic inheritance and its associated traditions. The prevalence of a gentry ethic significantly affected attitudes to trade and industry and shaped patterns of economic development. Business and the world of work was often despised, although wealth and the life-style it supported were naturally much appreciated. The position of people who held such views could only be maintained so long as others ran their properties and developed wealth for them. Capitalist activities and entrepreneurial development were, then, often left to the German and Jewish communities established throughout the region, a factor which made a distinctive contribution to the pattern of ethnic relations and their subsequent development. Czechs, Slovaks and most of the Balkans, on the other hand, had seen their native aristocracies destroyed by foreign conquerors. A different political and economic ethic tended to develop in these areas as modern societies were formed.

The Czechs thus developed an industrious bourgeoisie and educated middle class while, in the less developed south, elites of peasant origin retained strong links with the mass of the rural population. Such conditions also had a strong political impact, and they contributed to the strength of democratic constitutional tendencies in Bulgaria as it emerged from Ottoman rule following the Treaty of Berlin in 1878. But other forces were also at work. The crumbling of Ottoman power was a protracted one with varying national outcomes. The process of Turkish withdrawal and disentanglement from substantial parts of Eastern Europe lasted throughout the nineteenth century, beginning with Serbia's acquisition of a significant measure of autonomy in 1817 and the acquisition of full Greek independence in 1830. Differing forms of national identification grew and strengthened, with separate groups competing for local supremacy and claiming the same territory. Nationalist passions were running high by the end of the nineteenth century. The continued weakening of the Turkish empire led to the formation of competing new states and growing national tension, with two Balkan Wars breaking out in 1912 and 1913. Balkanisation, that is, the establishment of a patchwork of independent but antagonistic states, provided little satisfaction for competing national aspirations and no solution to the absence of an effective regional order.

Social change, population growth and instability

The combination of such historical developments with diverse currents of social change had a profound impact on the way in which the countries of Eastern Europe developed after 1918. This particularly concerned the different ways in which they worked out the problems arising from issues of social and ethnic identity. Pressures produced by the conditions endured by the rural-dwelling majority of the population and their problems in scraping together a livelihood added a second critical element. Nationalism and land reform thus emerged as the key issues of the region after the revolutions of 1848. Modernisation and diverse forms of social change gave rise to a wave of national opposition against the established political order, particularly when it was based on the older imperial forms. Population pressure made a further contribution and exacerbated existing problems of rural poverty, economic backwardness and land shortage. The population of major European powers like Britain, Russia and Germany roughly trebled during the nineteenth century, although that of France only grew by 43 per cent between 1801 and 1911. The high rate of population growth in Britain and Germany was accompanied by impressive levels of economic growth and industrial development, which meant that overall resources of national power increased significantly.

But the same could not be said of Russia where persistent problems of economic development continued through the nineteenth century and laid the basis for many of the instabilities and political conflicts of the twentieth. Elements of both of these patterns were reflected in developments in different parts of Eastern Europe. In general, though, it was the less stable combination of a rising population and unsteady economic growth seen in Russia that prevailed in Eastern Europe. In the Balkans, for example, population increases below the European average were recorded before 1880, but then saw growth rates considerably above it during the following years. Such uneven patterns of social change combined with the growth of national sentiments did much to create the rising tensions that underlay the outbreak both of the Balkan Wars and the more general European conflict that erupted in 1914. The solution arrived at with the armistice of 1918 was a military one, arrived at in no small measure with the assistance of the United States. But the region contained many tensions and areas of deep conflict. While the series of peace conferences and agreements tackled some of the problems, major challenges remained to face the new Eastern Europe that emerged in 1918.

3 The First World War and its Outcome

It was the First World War that was directly responsible for producing the conditions that finally enabled a new Eastern Europe to emerge and take concrete political form. For a lengthy period before the outbreak of the First World War in 1914 Turkey had been regarded as the 'sick man of Europe', and the extent of the territory it controlled in the Balkans as part of the Ottoman empire had been steadily shrinking. Virtually no one, however, foresaw that the unexpectedly protracted and bloody conflict would also spell the death of the Austro-Hungarian empire — and the defeat and territorial shrinkage both of Russia and Germany. The combined effect of these developments was to bring into existence a quite different Eastern Europe which was to persist, in a sequence of strikingly different forms, throughout the twentieth century. The immediate causes of the war lay with the inflamed ethnic tensions that smouldered throughout the Balkans. On 28 June 1914 Archduke Francis Ferdinand, heir to the Austro-Hungarian throne, was murdered in Sarajevo by the nationalist student Gavrilo Princip. A member of a secret Young Bosnia movement and of Serbian ethnic origin, he was seeking to promote the independence of Bosnia-Herzegovina from Austrian rule. Austria demanded full powers to pursue the killers and declared war on Serbia on 28 July when its government hesitated to grant them. The assassination soon sucked other states into the vortex of regional power politics and led to a general European war in early August just a few days after Austria's declaration of war on Serbia.

The conflict lasted far longer and was much more costly in terms of human and material resources than anyone had expected. The Russian empire was the first to crack and Tsar Nicholas II, the last representative of a Romanov dynasty that had ruled the steadily growing empire for 300 years, abdicated in February 1917 in the face of mounting revolutionary pressure. The United States of America entered the conflict on the side of the Allies later that year, and the Central Powers finally succumbed to growing Allied power in November 1918. Peace treaties were concluded with Hungary and the other defeated states in several locations around the French capital (at the Grand Trianon with Hungary, Neuilly with Bulgaria, and St Germain with Austrian republican representatives), although it was that signed with Germany in the hall of mirrors at Versailles, just outside Paris, which generally came to symbolise the post-war settlement.

The nature of the peace settlement

The main agreements were concluded in June 1919, even if by that date much of the territorial form of Eastern Europe had already been decided by the outcome of hostilities and disposition of military forces. Commitments made during the war to émigré groups provided for the formation of Czechoslovakia, while the favouring of Italian and Romanian interests also promised the radical dismemberment of the Austro-Hungarian empire. Proposals for a separate Polish state had also firmed up during the course of the war and, with the defeat of the German empire in the West, this also came to involve ethnically Polish areas that had formed part of Germany before 1914 as well as the former Congress Kingdom (established in 1815 after the Napoleonic wars) and other areas that had been under Russian domination.

Document: Address by Woodrow Wilson to US Congress, 11 February 1918.

The principles to be applied are these:

First, that each part of the final settlement must be based upon the essential justice of that particular case and upon such adjustments as are most likely to bring a peace that will be permanent;

Second, that peoples and provinces are not to be bartered about from sovereignty to sovereignty as if they were mere chattels and pawns in a game, even the great game, now forever discredited, of the balance of power; but that —

Third, every territorial settlement involved in this war must be made in the interest and for the benefit of the populations concerned, and not as a part of any mere adjustment or compromise of claims amongst rival states; and —

Fourth, that all well-defined national aspirations shall be accorded the utmost satisfaction that can be accorded them without introducing new or perpetuating old elements of discord and antagonism that would be likely in time to break the peace of Europe and consequently of the world.

The process of national liberation, proclaimed by US President Woodrow Wilson for all 'Slavs, Romanians and Czecho-Slovaks' in January 1917, before America's entry into the war, affirmed the ethnic basis of the East European state system after 1918, but in practice it was impossible to draw clear lines of division between the different nationalities. While Eastern Europe, for example, in the broad sense of the lands lying to the East of the predominantly German- and Italian-speaking areas covered roughly the same area as the Western portion of the Continent, it actually contained three times as many recognisably different nationalities as the other part. Most of them, too, often lived together with other ethnic groups and they did not fall neatly in separate areas of settlement. The twin objectives of a stable peace and national satisfaction enunciated by the Allies proved to be highly elusive.

Areas of tension and potential or actual conflict emerged from the word go, involving the margins of Bohemia-Moravia in Czechoslovakia, Upper Silesia (contested by Poland and Germany), the extensive borderlands of Poland and Russia (where military conflicts and war persisted until the signature of a treaty at Riga in March 1921), Transylvania and the Banat (transferred from Hungary to Yugoslavia), Slovakia, Istria (claimed both by Italy and Yugoslavia) and territories to the north of Trieste. The interests of Czechoslovakia were clearly favoured over those of Germans in the Sudetenland area of Bohemia and Moravia as well as those of Romania in Transylvania. Some issues were left for decision by plebiscite, these including the national status of Upper Silesia, parts of East Prussia, and Austrian areas bordering Slovenia and Hungary. Inhabitants of those areas were allowed to decide which country they should belong to. The interests of the 'successor' states to Austro-Hungary and those of (particularly) France, which unsurprisingly sought the weakening of Germany and diminution of its power, were clearly favoured. 1.25 million Germans were

The Peace Conference at Versailles, 1918

included in Poland, and 3.25 million Germans as well as 700,000 (Hungarian) Magyars in Czechoslovakia.

But Hungary was the country most severely affected by military defeat, losing three-fifths of its population and as much as two-thirds of its territory. 1.75 million Magyars were incorporated in Romania, and 500,000 in Yugoslavia. It was severely aggrieved by these losses and remained strongly revisionist throughout the inter-war period in terms of seeking to change the terms of the settlement imposed on it. Austrian imperial power was equally destroyed, but its population was more compact and thus less drawn into the ethnic conflicts that played such a large part in subsequent developments in Eastern Europe. Under these conditions Austrian attention was inevitably focused on the fate of the new German republic and the recuperation of its national power resources following the defeat of 1918. To this extent, the successor Austrian republic was divorced from the main concerns of Eastern Europe as understood in the context of this book.

Elsewhere, territorial disputes retained a high prominence and it was often the ethnic factor that emerged as the centre in such disputes. The former empires had indeed been composed of different ethnic groups, but ethnic affiliation was not the sole organising principle. Elements of traditional legitimacy and dynastic continuity were also called upon to justify imperial rule. With the promotion of the idea of national self-determination after 1918 ethnic considerations became that much more important, although national conflict might take different forms and there

A cartoon comment, in the Daily Express, *7 May 1919, on the imposed peace on Germany*

The nature of the peace settlement ●

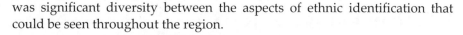

was significant diversity between the aspects of ethnic identification that could be seen throughout the region.

The East European state system

On the basis of war-time commitments made to various ethnic groups and Allied acceptance of the principle of national independence, the multi-national Austro-Hungarian empire was wholly dismantled. On this basis, and in combination with the shrinking territory of a now communist Russia and the withdrawal of a defeated Germany from its extended borders, a new Eastern Europe composed of diverse, formally independent states came into being. It was marked by the following dominant features:

- Poland, defeated and partitioned by its neighbours at the end of the eighteenth century, reappeared on the map of Europe;
- the new states of Czechoslovakia (made up of Czechs and Slovaks, as well as other national groups) and Yugoslavia (a federation of diverse 'south Slavs') were formed;
- Romania was considerably enlarged;
- the states of Lithuania, Latvia and Estonia were established on the Baltic coast in areas that had formed part of the Russian empire since the victory of Tsar Peter the Great over the Swedes in the 1710.

Thus, a whole new family of states had come into being between the now weakened powers of Germany and Russia, while the kaleidoscopic pattern of Balkan nationalities and state forms was given a further twist. The formation of new nation-states throughout the region and the emergence of an Eastern Europe in 1918 largely recast on ethnic lines was one of the most striking European outcomes of the First World War.

The region could be divided into different groups of states in terms of size and population:

- the largest were Poland, Romania, Czechoslovakia and Yugoslavia (between 27 and 12 million);
- considerably smaller were Hungary, Austria, Bulgaria, Greece and Finland (between 8 and 3 million);
- even smaller were the three mini-states of the Baltic region (Lithuania, Latvia and Estonia) and Albania (from 2.5 to 1 million).

Despite their formally national basis the new states were, too, ethnically quite diverse (see Table, page 23).

Eastern Europe, 1918-38

0 ——— 250
km

Tallinn

ESTONIA

SWEDEN

LATVIA

Riga

LITHUANIA

DENMARK

Copenhagen   *Baltic Sea*   Memel

Danzig   Kaunas   Wilno (Vilnius)   SOVIET UNION

EAST PRUSSIA

KRESY

River Vistula   *River Bug*

Berlin   Warsaw   Kiev

GERMANY   P O L A N D

VOLHYNIA

SUDATEN AREA   SILESIA   Lvov   GALACIA   *River Dniester*

Prague   Teschen   RUTHENIA   BESSARABIA

CZECHOSLOVAKIA   SLOVAKIA   *River Pruth*

River Danube   Vienna   Budapest   ROMANIA

AUSTRIA   HUNGARY   TRANSYLVANIA

SWITZ   Zagreb   VOJVODINA   BANAT   Bucharest

Belgrade

YUGOSLAVIA   BULGARIA

ITALY   *Adriatic Sea*   KOSOVO   Sofia   T U R K E Y

Rome   ALBANIA

Tirana   GREECE

National population and major ethnic minorities in Eastern Europe

	Population (millions)	Total minorities (per cent)	Major groups
Poland	27.177	30.8	Ukrainian (Ruthenian), Jewish, Belorussian, German.
Romania (1930)	18.057	28.1	Hungarian, German, Jewish, Ukrainian, Russian, Bulgarian.
Czechoslovakia *	13.613	34.5	German, Hungarian, Ruthenian (Ukrainian), Jewish.
Yugoslavia *	11.985	25.5	Slovene, German, Hungarian, Albanian, Romanian.
Hungary	7.990	10.5	German, Slovak, Croatian.
Bulgaria	4.847	16.6	Turkish, Gypsy, Greek.

*National statistics contained a single category for Czechs and Slovaks in Czechoslovakia, Serbs, Croats, Macedonians and Muslims (Bosniaks) in Yugoslavia.

Origins of the new states

The origins of the new states were similarly varied, and this was a factor that subsequently influenced their alignment on the international scene: Czechoslovakia and Yugoslavia were new states whose formation had been agreed by the Allies during the course of the war. Albania was also recently established (largely to deny Serbia access to the Adriatic sea), having gained international recognition as an independent state in 1913 on the verge of the outbreak of war. Bulgaria and Romania had emerged as increasingly autonomous powers in the nineteenth century with the decline of Turkish power, but now saw their borders once again reformed as part of the post-war settlement after years of continuing territorial change (most recently during the Balkan Wars of 1912 and 1913). Bulgaria had fought with the central powers and was the first of them to be defeated, losing territory to Romania, Greece and — to a lesser extent — Yugoslavia. Romania also gained the major area of Transylvania from Hungary (across the southern Carpathians), the smaller territory of Bukovina from Austria as another defeated enemy, and Bessarabia from a Russia in 1919 that was still struggling with military defeat, revolution and civil war. Poland, on the other hand, had a more established record as a European territorial entity and saw itself restoring an historic identity as an independent nation following the partition of the former state at the end of the eighteenth century between Russia, Prussia and Austria.

Of the four largest states in the region, then, two (Czechoslovakia and Yugoslavia) were new creations, one (Poland) was a modern reconstitution of the old commonwealth, with only Romania having existed in something like its post-war form (although considerably smaller and a limited history of statehood) before 1914. The formation of the Baltic states represented the achievement of a form of autonomous national life with far more slender historical roots, these being stronger in the case of Lithuania which had entered into a form of political union with Poland as early as 1386. Finland, on the northern fringe of Eastern Europe and under the Swedish monarchy until 1809, experienced varying degrees of autonomy under Russia before it proclaimed independence in 1917. Hungary, on the other hand, suffered the fate of a defeated central power and emerged in 1918 as a diminished rump state, having enjoyed only a relatively brief period of regional pre-eminence within the dual monarchy of Austria-Hungary established in 1867. Together with Austria and Bulgaria, the other defeated and territorially reduced states of post-1918 Eastern Europe, it now appeared as one of the medium-size countries of the region.

Nationality in Eastern Europe

Eastern Europe after the First World War was nationally and culturally diverse and differentiated by a wide range of social, economic and historic factors. The 'national principle', was generally applied where possible, which meant as a broad rule (widely diverged from in practice) that separate ethnic groups were grouped into independent states where they formed most of the population. This was thought to provide a good basis for holding the new territorial units together in a reasonably democratic and peaceful way and to dampen down the hostility and antagonisms that had been all too obvious throughout the region before the First World War. The national principle was thus believed to be the best chance of securing the viability of the new states. It was, however, patchily implemented and, when the nations identified seemed to be just too small to provide a basis for the establishment of a modern state, two or more were joined together (as in Czechoslovakia and in Yugoslavia) to produce a more viable unit.

One way of distinguishing nationalities was through linguistic differences. Much of Eastern Europe is populated by Slavs, although Hungary, Romania and Albania are clear exceptions and their dominant ethnic group speaks a non-Slavonic language. But many of the Slavonic languages recognised as separate tongues in the twentieth century had a relatively recent identity and were often formalised as the very idea of nationhood took shape in Eastern Europe. The language that predominated in the nineteenth century did not necessarily reflect any coherent ethnic or racial identity and many people were bilingual, often speaking two languages which they mainly used in different contexts like home and business. Official nationalities did not necessarily represent very strong or well entrenched traditions. In inter-war Polish statistics some people are just classified as 'local' because that is how they saw themselves, just not belonging to any single broader category. The modern nations which are recorded as emerging so distinctively and confidently during the nineteenth century in fact represented a selection from a range of historical possibilities.

Such modern nations were, in fact, following the title of an influential book, 'imagined communities' constructed in the midst of the turbulent social change that followed the beginnings of modernisation in Eastern Europe. While often defined and their details fleshed out by intellectuals, the values they represented were those eagerly sought by a much larger popular mass. They generally embodied a mythic idea of solidarity and mutual loyalty that stood in clear contrast to the harsh conditions and insecurity of people's lives (although they often had little chance of being realised in the future, either). Movements based on such principles were much more effective in defining an enemy and directing activity against it than in establishing or maintaining the national community they claimed to represent. But, while unsullied national identity is as misleading a notion as racial purity, such uncertainty did not prevent the emergence of confidently articulated political principles and the rapid growth of social movements associated with them. Whatever the roots of ethnic, linguistic and national differences in Eastern Europe at the beginning of the twentieth century there can be little doubt that the principle of national identity had gained considerable strength in the international community by 1918 and was a factor that played a major role in conceptions of the state system proposed by the war-time victors to replace the multi-national arrangements held in place by the former empires.

Aspects of regional diversity

There were, in fact, several major factors that divided the new Eastern Europe, some considerably more important than nationality in many people's eyes. Economic development and the growth of industrial strength had become a highly significant characteristic of the modern European state. Against a general background of rural poverty, the Czech lands of Bohemia and Moravia were well developed with the factories and industrial centres quite absent from the territories of Bulgaria and Albania. The Czech lands — an area of Slavic settlement that extended into the surrounding German areas — had been the most industrialised portion of the Austro-Hungarian empire as a whole. In the early years of the new Eastern Europe after the First World War, therefore, it was only in Czechoslovakia that the peasantry did not constitute the majority of the population. 34 per cent of the population resided in rural areas there, but in Hungary 55 per cent and in Poland 63 per cent lived in the countryside. In Bulgaria as much as 80 per cent of the population was rural. There was, as might be expected, insufficient land to meet the demand of this large and — by the early twentieth century — rapidly growing group of country-dwellers. Poland was fairly typical of the region and had, in 1921, 65 per cent of all land in holdings no larger than five hectares. The large group of peasant farmers this represented, more than half of all those who held some land, occupied no more than 15 per cent of the arable land area as a whole. Even in Czechoslovakia, where the rural population was smaller, 44 per cent of farm-holdings were of less than two hectares (which comprised 7 per cent of agricultural land).

The differing levels of wealth and economic development were often associated with other distinctive features. Religious faith also provided a highly potent source of social identity. Poland, Czechoslovakia, Hungary and Lithuania were mainly Catholic, while Estonia and Latvia were committed to the Lutheran form of Protestantism. In the generally impoverished Balkans, Bulgaria, Romania and much of Yugoslavia held to the alternative rites of the Orthodox Church, while Albania was mostly Moslem. Life under former imperial rulers had played a large part in establishing such differences, with Bosnian Moslems having converted to the religion of the Ottoman conquerors — although Serbs held tenaciously to their Orthodox beliefs. The even more ancient division between Catholic and Greek Orthodox reflected the fact that many East Europeans had received their Christian faith from Catholic Rome in contrast to the Orthodox variant promulgated from Constantinople, an echo of the administrative division of the Roman Empire made by Diocletian in the fourth century AD to help administration and strengthen its defences. More than a thousand years were to elapse from this date to the capture of Constantinople (later Istanbul) by the Turks in 1453. Modern differences between Catholic Croats and Orthodox Serbs, nevertheless, still reflected the ancient divide.

Internal divisions within the region were also enhanced by the fact that the post-1918 states, some of them newly created as modern national or multi-national entities, had previously formed part of different empires and fought on different sides in the First World War (or, in the case of Poland, was formed of groups who had fought on opposing sides). In terms of political character, several of the post-war states were monarchies, generally of a rather unstable kind, while the newly formed states of Czechoslovakia, Poland and the Baltic area were republics. Awareness of national tradition was another important factor. Although in modern form a new republic, Poland was one of the region's historic nations whose traditions and culture as a national community extended back nearly a thousand years. On the side of the vanquished in the First World War, Hungarians had a comparable history and depth of national feeling which intensified their feelings of loss and resentment throughout the inter-war period. While Czechoslovakia was also a new state in its modern multi-national form, it included most of the 'historic provinces' of Bohemia, Moravia and Silesia identified with the Crown of St Wenceslas in the tenth century (he is still remembered in the famous carol every year for having looked out on the Christmas snow). While some of the states of post-First World War Eastern Europe had the bright stamp of the twentieth century on their structures, then, the traditions and culture of many of those who lived within them were quite ancient. The Eastern Europe created after the First World War was highly diverse and contained many obstacles to the establishment both of viable nation-states and a stable regional order.

Points to note

* The peace settlement arrived at after the First World War was intended to satisfy the national aspirations of the peoples of Eastern Europe but in fact left many unsatisfied groups throughout the region.
* After 1918 the old continental empires of Germany, Austria-Hungary and Russia were dismantled, and a more diverse state system including the new countries of Czechoslovakia and Yugoslavia and a restored Poland created.
* The national principle was not applied consistently in the creation of the new states, with some states formed by the addition of two or more distinct ethnic groups and others containing substantial minorities.
* Other forms of social division contributed to the diversity of the region, particularly those based on levels of economic development, religion, political heritage and national tradition.

4 State Building and Problems of National Democracy in the 1920s

Independence and democracy

The principles on which modern Eastern Europe was established after the First World War were those of liberal democracy and national independence. For the first time since the Middle Ages many of the major nationalities of the region gained their independence and shared, in general terms, the form of government that was dominant in Western Europe. All broadly followed the dual focus on nationalism and democracy set in the violent upheavals of the French Revolution but encountered great problems in combining the two features. In Eastern Europe the mix of nationalities sparked off numerous international and domestic conflicts. Tensions between the new states, based on a rich array of multiple ethnic identities and loyalties, soon dominated much of the regional political agenda and undermined rather than strengthened processes of national integration and state formation. The views of those like Tomáš Masaryk, the founder of Czechoslovakia, proved to be remarkably optimistic in terms of the behaviour of individual states and the nature of the international framework in which they operated.

Document: Extract from T. Masaryk, *The World Revolution* (1925).

The Peace Treaties have created more just conditions throughout Europe, and we are entitled to expect that the tension between States and races will decrease. Despite all antagonisms, there is, moreover, ground for hope that the lessons of the war will strengthen the prospects for peace. What may be faulty in the new order will be susceptible of pacific adjustment as occasion arises. All difficulties notwithstanding, it is possible to detect the beginnings of a free federalisation of Europe in place of the absolutist mastery of one Great Power or of alliances of Great Powers, over the Continent. In a new Europe of this kind the independence of even the smallest national individuality can be safeguarded; and the League of Nations suggests an instructive analogy to what a united Europe may become ... The history of Europe since the eighteenth century proves that, given democratic freedom, little peoples can gain independence. The World War was the climax of the movement begun by the French Revolution, a movement that liberated one oppressed people after another, and now there is a chance for a democratic Europe and for the freedom and independence of all her nations.

❧﮿⌇❀ —— The 1920s   State Building and its Problems

The countries of the region faced major problems of economic consolidation and development within the newly formed national boundaries. Social inequalities were pronounced, and the dominance of a large group of poverty-stricken country-dwellers in the less developed South and East recalled more the social contrasts of eighteenth-century pre-revolution France than the class conflicts of contemporary Western Europe. The range of political, ethnic and economic demands posed major challenges to the authority of newly installed national leaders and severely tested their capacity to satisfy the recently awakened expectations of the citizens of the new states. Early hopes of democratic development were mostly soon disappointed, and by the end of the 1920s anti-democratic practices and forms of dictatorship were well on the way to becoming entrenched throughout much of the region.

Political tensions and new state structures

As the nationality issue was so important in the new Eastern Europe, it is useful to see how relations between national groups fell into different patterns across the countries of the region. Some new states were explicitly associated with particular national groups which had not previously identified themselves in such exclusive political terms before; they were 'state-nations' in a sense not previously seen. It was only just prior to the partition of Poland at the end of the eighteenth century that anything like a Polish national community began to emerge in political terms, for example. The state that emerged in 1918 was founded on modern principles and with an emotional appeal quite different from that of its feudalistic predecessor. Throughout Eastern Europe groups not identified with the 'state-nation' in which they lived now clearly emerged as ethnic minorities (Jews, Germans, and — in the Balkans — the Greeks). Yet others were distinct both from the majority national group and the obvious minorities, constituting a third category. They were by no means a dominant nationality but were not marginal either — Slovaks and Croats fell into this category in terms of their self-perceived subordinate relationship with, respectively, Czechs in Czechoslovakia and the Serbs in Yugoslavia. Further tensions, although less severe, emerged within ethnic groups that had previously formed part of different empires or political units. A unified Poland, for example, had to be constructed by Poles who had previously lived within the borders of three different foreign empires.

But while very prominent, ethnic differences were by no means the only basis for political conflict in post-1918 Eastern Europe. Class inequality and great disparities in living standards were also prominent in a region which faced enormous problems of economic development from a very low economic base. The wealthy elite was proportionately very small and surrounded by a population in a state mostly of extreme poverty, particularly in the countryside. Some areas were, nevertheless, marked by extensive economic development and stood at a relatively advanced stage of industrialisation, which provided conditions for the appearance of organised forms of class struggle and more effective political opposition, tendencies strengthened by recently acquired national independence and new possibilities for political expression. The formal framework for this combustible political mixture was, however, provided by liberal democratic institutions derived from West European models and constitutions largely based on the form of the Third French Republic.

A number had dominant legislatures with a relatively weak executive. Parliaments had much opportunity for discussion and law-making but generally little capacity for carrying out their decisions, a situation tailored to produce disappointed expectations and growing frustration all round. The Polish presidency was deliberately weakened to prevent the emergence of strong leadership by particular interests. Others (Romania, Bulgaria and Yugoslavia) were monarchies in which parliaments also became the key political arena. Hungary, too, initially had a democratic constitution while formally remaining a monarchy, which left it with the right to claim the historic lands associated with the Crown of St Stephen. No satisfactory incumbent was ever found for the post. Hungary, indeed, typified many of the contradictions of Eastern Europe during this period: it was a nation-state, where a third of the nation lived outside its border; a kingdom which never found a monarch (the proprietor of the *Daily Mail*, Lord Rothermere, was reported to be one unlikely candidate for the post); and a land-locked country whose permanent ruler between the wars was an admiral. It soon became obvious that the establishment of the kind of formal institutions that prevailed in Western Europe and the United States, and generally worked there quite well, was not enough to guarantee either democratic practice or stability in Eastern Europe.

The prospects for western-style democracy taking root in Eastern Europe were not good. It was certainly optimistic to expect, as the Western powers — and particularly US President Wilson — seemed to, that liberal democracy was a viable form of government that could be expected to flourish in a region of newly established states characterised by deep national and social divisions and thus sharp political tensions, where experience of any constitutional political activity was extremely limited, and where literacy and educational levels were also low. The relevance of the constitutional model generally adopted was doubtful in terms of the primacy it assigned to legislative powers rather than those of a strong executive. A less sophisticated but more effective governing structure would have been more appropriate for the newly formed states in giving their leaders the means to achieve basic objectives and deal rapidly with the basic tasks of state formation. A clearer idea of the problems faced by the new states in operating a complex democratic system may be gained by considering some more recent cases. The newly independent states of Africa after the Second World War were, for example, in something of a similar situation and their newly established democratic systems also turned out to be very short-lived.

But neither would a simpler form of political arrangement with stronger leadership capacity necessarily have strengthened their democratic prospects. The high degree of centralisation that was generally involved in the new state structures did not help, for example, as it hardly smoothed the path to dealings with the numerous ethnic minorities. But in practice constitutional issues and the precise nature of the institutions established in the new states were largely beside the point. Early conflicts between contending political forces over concrete goals generally tended to dominate political life in the new states. Violent confrontations between competing groups and the adoption of emergency measures often overrode the formal constitutional arrangements within which political processes were supposed to take place, thus weakening the basis of the new regimes before they had any real chance to become stabilised.

Hungary

Political instability and social turmoil continued throughout Eastern Europe even when hostilities between the major contending powers ended in November 1918. Borders were fluid, and hopes and expectations of the post-war order often unrealistically high. This affected both those on the winning side and defeated nations, particularly when they faced a highly uncertain future. Amidst the defeated nations, Hungary was subject to a particularly high degree of territorial and political instability. With the collapse of the Russian war effort Romania was initially roundly defeated by the Central Powers (Germany and Austria-Hungary), although it was later able to re-enter the fray. Far from facing any loss of territory at this point, Hungary actually gained some from Romania by the Peace of Bucharest concluded in May 1918. Even some months later the Hungarian establishment was unwilling to contemplate defeat and hoped to lay responsibility for the war on its Germanic comrades in arms. Such stubborn optimism on the part of the conservative leadership did not last long. A revolt of Budapest workers and the disaffection of the military caused a change of leadership, and in October Count Károlyi was appointed premier. Károlyi was a noted liberal with established democratic views. But his accession to power came far too late to dissuade the Western Allies from their determination to punish the country for its joint war responsibility with the Austrians. They were now also committed to rewarding the smaller nationalities of the empire at the expense of the defeated powers.

Under strong Allied military pressure, increasing areas of former Hungarian territory had to be given up. Károlyi's position became increasingly untenable and, in March 1919, he resigned in the face of yet another territorial demand in favour of Romania from the Allied representative in Budapest, the French Lieutenant Colonel Vyx. Hungary was shown little sympathy by the victorious powers and Károlyi did not receive any sympathy from the West in his attempt to preserve the country's post-war position. Together with the Socialists who formed a major part of his coalition he had looked to Russia, itself the site of tumultuous revolutionary struggles, as the only possible source of support. Although by no means revolutionary themselves, the Socialists now took power and released from prison the communists who had been imprisoned just a month earlier. Under the leadership of Béla Kun, a pre-war functionary of the Socialist Party and former journalist, a Soviet Hungarian Republic was established on Russian lines. (A constitution basing power on the workers' *soviets* — or councils — was also adopted by communist Russia in 1918. The whole area under Russian communist control became the Soviet Union in 1923.)

Kun rejected the Vyx memorandum and expanded the army above the number permitted by the Allies. By such measures, surprisingly enough, he won the passive support of the entrenched Hungarian conservative and reactionary forces. But communist economic and social policies were not generally popular. The peasants were refused land reform as the communist programme called for the eventual collectivisation of agriculture, and they had much of their food produce commandeered to feed the towns and military forces. Nationalisation policies were imposed on trade and industry and met with a mixed reception in Hungarian society as a whole. Radical social policies like the prohibition of child labour, improved educational opportunities, sexual equality and wage increases met with more wide-spread approval. But Kun's government had no domestic power base and little time to contemplate building one. It was also rejected and roundly criticised by the Western Powers. The Soviet Republic in fact only lasted 133 days. The Romanian army advanced into Hungarian territory on 16 April 1919 and met surprisingly strong Hungarian resistance, with the communist government finally capitulating on 1 August.

There followed a 'White Terror' in which known and alleged communists were ruthlessly persecuted, and severe punishment visited on workers and peasants who had collaborated with them. Jews were widely attacked in actions that recalled the pogroms of medieval times in which Christians persecuted Jews and destroyed their communities. At least 5,000 people died overall and 70,000 were imprisoned. Elections were held in March 1920 and Admiral Miklós Horthy became Regent with the emphatic support of the pre-war elite. He had extensive powers over both parliament and government, and also retained control over the army (which gave him a sufficiently strong base to enable him to retain power until removed in the wake of the German invasion in 1944). After the elections of 1920, in which 40 per cent of the population had been able to participate, a return to pre-war legislation was enacted in which only 27.5 per cent of the population had the vote and ballots were largely open rather than secret. This ensured the permanent rule of the Unity Party, which was in fact more of a governmental and administrative agency than a political party as understood in the West European sense.

Austria

The optimistic early steps taken towards democracy in Hungary were thus soon followed by the revolutionary Soviet interlude and a return to the highly restrictive and conservative form of rule strongly reminiscent of the pre-war system. In the other part of the former empire many Austrians did not see a viable future for the equally truncated Austrian state, and moves were initially made to join with the new German republic. The Western Allies did not allow this. After the introduction of a democratic constitution in September 1920 the country was governed by diverse coalitions of the Catholic and increasingly conservative Christian Social Party and the German Nationalists. The power of the radical Social Democrats was largely restricted to the trade unions and the capital of Vienna, where far-reaching decentralisation gave them extensive powers.

This tenuous political stability did not last long, and divisions widened between the competing camps. Both democracy and national stability were threatened by intensifying conflicts between the German nationalist *Heimwehr* (Home Defence Force) and an equivalent socialist defence organisation. A tenuous democracy was maintained under the Christian Social Democrat Englebert Dolfuss, who remained resolutely opposed to the Socialists while coming under increasing pressure from the German Nationalists and a rapidly growing Nazi movement. Conflict grew as Hitler's position strengthened in Germany and the Weimar Republic entered its final phase (see page 57). Although Dollfuss was killed in a failed Nazi *putsch* in 1934, some prospects for the continuation of Austrian independence were maintained under former minister of education Kurt Schuschnigg. But by this stage the government could make little claim to authentic democracy. Both Social Democrats and the trade unions had been banned, and a corporatist constitution on Mussolini's Fascist model adopted, before the death of Dollfuss. Although the Austrian state survived for a few more years until 1938 it was run on strongly authoritarian lines.

Poland

The establishment of liberal democracy was hardly any easier or more successful in the restored Polish Republic. Polish borders were subject to continuing uncertainty, particularly in the East. The emerging state faced not just a defeated and internally warring Russia but also newly re-established Lithuania (which contested Wilno/Vilnius, a city of great historic importance to both nations) and the Ukraine, which was also seeking to establish its independence. At the end of the war Polish military leader, Józef Piłsudski, imprisoned by the Germans in 1917, was now well placed to declare independence. This he did in November 1918 and held power until the return to Poland from America of Ignace Paderewski, the renowned concert pianist, whose talent for harmony was now directed to overcoming the fratricidal political tensions that persisted between different nationalist groups. They succeeded in forming a provisional national government in January 1919. The Allies were unsure about which contender they should favour and were content to settle for a compromise leaving, in January 1919, Piłsudski as head of state, with Paderewski becoming premier and Dmowski as the Polish representative at the forthcoming peace conference.

Piłsudski was undoubtedly the dominant figure in newly independent Poland. He had a lengthy record both as a socialist and, even more emphatically, a nationalist who saw liberation from Russia as Poland's main task and the formation of a powerful multi-national state (including Ukrainians, Bielorussians and Lithuanians under Polish leadership) as the best guarantee of national independence. It was as head of state and military commander that he launched the Polish-Soviet war of 1920 in pursuit of this vision. He was passionately admired and respected by many Poles — but also bitterly attacked by Roman Dmowski and the National

'The new Polish cabinet holds its first meeting' published in Le Canard Enchaîné, *Paris in 1928. This cartoon comments on the military nature of Polish government after Piłsudski's 1926 coup*

Democrats as an archaic romantic. Dmowski saw Prussia as the main agency of Poland's destruction and Germany as its major enemy. He was therefore more inclined to collaborate with Russia to further Polish interests. Dmowski's vision was of a nationally cohesive Poland and he saw only a subordinate place for ethnic minorities within it, amongst whom he included the Jewish population. Fundamentally different concepts of the new Polish state, its strategic interests and ethnic basis were, therefore, well established from the outset. The existence of different political currents remained at the heart of the politics of independent Poland. Such differences split the political class, national leadership and the army from the outset. They influenced the way in which key institutions of the new state like the presidency were formed and affected the prospects of democratic development in various ways.

While Piłsudski was head of state from 1918 to 1922, the constituent assembly was dominated by National Democrats and they made sure that the powers of the president established in the new constitution remained weak. This dissuaded Piłsudski from standing for election to the office and had the effect of weakening the legitimacy of the constitution in the eyes of his followers. The diversity of political groups and traditions in the new state also fed straight into the new legislature by virtue of the system of proportional representation employed in elections, which led to continuing political fragmentation and instability. From the declaration of independence in 1918 until 1926 there were 14 different governments. After President Narutowicz was elected in November 1922 he was promptly assassinated the following month. His assassin was a nationalist aggrieved that the right-wing parliamentary majority had been overridden by an opposing coalition which included national minorities (not least the Jews).

Political passions did not die down in the following years, nor was stability established in national life. Although removed from political life, too, Piłsudski's influence over the army remained undiminished. On this basis he intervened politically in May 1926 to mount a *coup*, with the support of the Socialists, to forestall the formation of a further right-dominated coalition. This, he and his allies felt, was likely to cause yet more disruption. Piłsudski's proclaimed objective was to stabilise political life and improve Polish parliamentarism rather than overthrow democracy. The fighting was not extensive and lasted only three days, but Piłsudski's command over the army proved unassailable. After reasonably unconstrained elections in 1928, though, centre, left-wing and peasant party forces were increasingly harassed. A more repressive authoritarian regime was installed following considerably more restrictive elections held in November 1930. The weaknesses of parliamentary government were being made good, it seemed, by securing its virtual abolition and the progressive elimination of democratic rights. Issues of nationality and ethnic tensions clearly entered into the problematic course of Poland's new democracy. The key tensions, though, actually developed within the different camps of the Polish political community. It was the competing visions of Polish national development that underlay the weak democracy of the new Polish state.

Yugoslavia

A different picture emerged in the new, and explicitly multinational, states established elsewhere in Eastern Europe. Particularly intractable problems were created by the national tensions that developed in the newly established Yugoslavia. The ethnic pluralism of the country was summed up in its original name: the Kingdom of the Serbs, Croats and Slovenes. The name Yugoslavia itself simply referred to south Slavs, a category which did not itself actually indicate any concrete social identity. Their languages were related, and those of Serbs and Croats virtually identical. But the nationalities differed with respect to religion, imperial background and overall political vision — Serbs looking primarily towards Russia, while Croats and Slovenes directed their gaze steadfastly to the West (although even here there had been a difference between the Hungarian and Austrian affiliations of the two groups).

Free elections in November 1920 created a large majority for the Croat Peasant Party in that part of the country, but there was a split vote in Serbia between the Radicals of Nikola Pašić (who were in fact increasingly conservative) and Ljuba Davidović's Democrats. Pašić generally held the premiership, as he already had during the world war, and the Croat Peasants shifted between positions of general co-operation and collaboration — and sometimes alliance with Davidović's opposition party. The Slovenes were given a large measure of autonomy to keep them in the Serbian-dominated coalition, while equivalent concessions were made to the Bosnian Moslems with respect to land reform. Pašić died in December 1926. Elections now confirmed the growing polarisation of Yugoslav political life between the Serbian centre and a Croat-led camp which pursued a policy of decentralisation. Albanian and Macedonian minorities and other forces also supported this line. The mood of ethnic confrontation also grew increasingly violent. In June 1928 a Radical deputy from Montenegro drew a pistol in parliament. He shot two Croat deputies dead and fatally wounded the Croat leader, Radić. By the end of the year the governing coalition had collapsed. Yugoslavia's tenuous parliamentary democracy had run into a dead end. With no solution in sight to the struggle between the warring national camps, in January 1929 King Alexander imposed a royal dictatorship.

Albania

Violence was equally close to the surface of political life in the even newer political creation that was the Albanian state. Prospects there for the emergence of anything like a viable democracy were negligible. In what was probably the most backward corner of Europe, formal government was maintained until August 1920 by Italian forces. A sequence of governments then followed in which Ahmed Zogolli was a regular participant. He became prime minister in 1922 at the age of 27 and changed his name to Zogu, which had the advantage of sounding less Turkish and more Albanian. In 1924 he was shot and wounded, an event soon followed by the murder of a major political opponent. A *coup* was launched by another competitor, but he, too, was overthrown, in December 1924. Zogu was nominated to a strengthened presidency and, in 1928, assumed the throne as King Zog. His powers over the country were further strengthened and national security generally enhanced by the conclusion of a pact with Italy. The experience of the young Albania was not marked by any degree of democratic achievement, nor did it show much capacity to develop an independent national existence.

Czechoslovakia

In contrast to Yugoslavia, the other multi-national experiment conducted in Eastern Europe with the establishment of the new state of Czechoslovakia was considerably more successful. In socio-economic terms there could be little greater contrast in the early twentieth century between the highly developed areas of Bohemia and Moravia in the West of Czechoslovakia and the poverty-stricken peasant lands of Albania and Serbia. At issue here was not just the question of wealth but also the broader framework of social structure, literacy, education and social organisation — all features that encourage and support the development of parliamentary government and democratic practices. Less strain was, therefore, brought to bear on ethnic relations. Neither were the divisions between Czechs and Slovaks as sharp as those in Yugoslavia in terms of religion, imperial heritage or administrative practice. The position of the large German minority in the largely Slav Czechoslovak state was another matter, although the main issue here was the relationship with a humiliated and resentful Germany which was to provide conditions for the rise of the lethal Nazi movement there. Nevertheless, a distinctly anti-German policy was pursued in Czechoslovakia from the outset. In March 1919 Czech troops shot over 50 Germans during street demonstrations.

But no part of the new state's population was driven by the same kind of intense nationalism that the Serbs held close to their hearts. The Czechs had already received extensive civic rights within Austria-Hungary, and before 1914 they had mostly sought to extend these freedoms rather than establish a new state. Slovaks had harboured even fewer thoughts of developing any form of national independence. But, as the war progressed, a prominent Czech group led by Tomáš Masaryk saw the dangers of victory on the part of the Central Powers. He feared the influence in central Europe of a victorious German nationalism and the encouragement it would give to the more conservative forces in Austria-Hungary. Masaryk therefore began to work for a Czecho-Slovak partnership to guard against the threat the Central Powers might pose. Only in June 1918 did Masaryk reach an agreement about the form of a future state with representatives of the large Slovak population in the United States. The Pittsburgh agreement concluded there provided for extensive autonomy on the part of the Slovak population. Few, however, were actually qualified or were adequately trained to make full use of the opportunities when the new state was established. Within the new economic context of the post-war period, too, Slovaks were deprived of their former economic links with Hungarian centres and were disadvantaged by the need to forge new relations of trade and unemployment. They were also resentful of the centralisation of key economic activities around the Czech areas of the new federal state.

Their critical sentiments found greatest expression in the rising vote for the Slovak People's Party led by Father Hlinka. This was particularly apparent between the elections of 1920 and 1925. The clerical nature of the party also channelled a certain measure of resentment felt about the secular character of the Czechoslovak state and generally reflected elements of a pro-independence nature. But any such opposition stayed well within the bounds of the democratic order. In marked distinction to the Polish record, the new constitution adopted in February 1920 created a strong executive which gave formal backing to the personal authority of Masaryk as head of state. Any revolutionary tendencies within the strong communist party that now existed were easily contained within an effectively operating political system. The major Slovak and German parties both joined the governing coalition. Major ethnic divisions did not, therefore, lead in this case to the political fracturing of the newly established multinational states but to the evolution of arrangements made explicitly to avoid this.

Bulgaria

National considerations were of great significance for political developments in Bulgaria. Set in the poor peasant areas of the southern Balkans with little experience of self-government or constitutional politics, it is hardly surprising that Bulgaria followed a pattern marked more by the intransigence and violent conflict seen in Yugoslavia and Albania than the more co-operative relations that had developed in Czechoslovakia. Like Hungary, Bulgaria's status as a defeated power caused a critical loss of confidence in the existing leadership. The country had, too, been involved in the two Balkan wars of 1912-13 and had a lengthy history of recent conflict. The defeat of 1918 opened the way to major political change. In August 1919 power was handed to Alexander Stamboliiski, long-standing leader of the peasant movement. He had opposed war with Russia and had been imprisoned for this stand during the hostilities. A radical agrarian and promoter of peasant interests, he won a second electoral victory in 1920 (most significantly over the communists) and began a major programme of land reform by abolishing the few large estates that remained in Bulgaria.

When he won a further substantial victory in the elections of April 1923, a number of opponents and established groups whose interests he had affronted planned violent action against the agrarians' government. Amidst the protracted international negotiations of the early post-war period he had also made strenuous efforts to improve relations with Yugoslavia over the contested lands of Macedonia. But he had little in the way of a domestic power basis apart from peasant electoral support. Under these conditions Stamboliiski was overthrown and murdered in June 1923 in the course of a military *coup*. Tortured and mutilated by Macedonian fanatics, his head was sent off to the capital, Sofia, in a biscuit tin. Having stood aside from the original *coup* the communists then rose against the government. When this failed, the new government proceeded to pursue a policy of terroristic repression against all left-wing forces. This further intensified after the communists attempted to assassinate the King by placing a bomb in a Sofia cathedral. Against this background, foreign pressure brought about the resignation of premier Tsankov in January 1926. Developments between 1923 and 1925 saw the elimination of the left from Bulgarian politics and confirmed the effective end of the country's brief attempt at democracy.

Violence was never far from the surface and throughout much of the post-war period a major influence over government and national political life was exercised by the Internal Macedonian Revolutionary Organisation (IMRO). The group aimed by any means possible to bring about the restoration of Bulgarian control over the fiercely contested region. Bulgarian rule over Macedonia had been temporarily achieved in the First Balkan War, and once more when Bulgaria entered the general European conflict in 1915. IMRO continued to operate from Bulgarian territory throughout the 1920s and was a major destabilising factor both domestically and in the international politics of the Balkan region. The replacement of Tsankov as prime minister by Andrei Lipachev, a Macedonian, meant that no concerted action was taken against IMRO throughout the rest of the 1920s. Bulgaria, nevertheless, held further, relatively open elections during 1931. A People's Bloc was voted into power and was able to implement some effective measures designed to cope with the effects of the depression. In a move not dissimilar to Piłsudski's *coup* in Poland, though (see page 35), a military-based group again seized power in 1934 and put a final end to parliamentary and party politics.

Greece

Although very much on the margins of Eastern Europe, Greece had been equally shaken by conflicts with its Balkan neighbours during the Balkan Wars (not least with Bulgaria over the Macedonian question), indecision about intervention in the First World War, and the dominant struggle with

Turkey. This was one sphere of conflict in which the Turks were victorious and Greece suffered a decisive and dramatic defeat in the aftermath of the First World War. Smyrna (Izmir) on the Turkish mainland had been settled by Greeks since ancient times and it contained a Greek population of nearly half a million in 1914. After the war the town and surrounding area were handed over to Greek jurisdiction, but further attempts to re-establish a Greek empire on the eastern coast of the Aegean were strongly resisted by Turkish nationalist forces. Smyrna was retaken in August 1922, all Greeks expelled or killed, and the town set alight. This spelt an ignominious end to the ambitious Greek hopes of re-establishing an empire throughout the Aegean in the wake of the defeated Ottomans. Apart from the large numbers massacred or killed in military operations, Greeks expelled from Turkish areas made up nearly a fifth of the mainland population in the 1920s.

The debacle led to the overthrow of the monarchy by republican army officers and the execution of a number of prominent politicians. Military defeat led once more to the destruction of most remaining hopes of democratic development. The constitution of 1911 allowed for parliamentary government, but few signs of stable democratic practice emerged and successive kings were closely involved in politics. The republican *coup* led by Colonel Plastiras in 1924 did not succeed in achieving any stability and a new dictatorship was installed by General Pangalos in 1926 which was, indeed, followed by yet further unrest. The brief period of rule by Pangalos was succeeded by a number of governments, in most of which the influence of former prime minister Venizelos was prominent and helped achieve some stability.

Romania

Prior to the First World War the political system in Romania had been strongly monarchical, more similar to British practice in the early eighteenth century than the contemporary West European model whose operation was suggested by its constitution. The *jacquerie* of 1907, a massive peasant uprising in which over 10,000 lost their lives, nevertheless demonstrated the clear need for change and certain reforms were already contemplated before the death of King Carol I in October 1914. Despite an unimpressive military performance, Romania more than doubled its area and population as a result of the war. All Romanian men were allowed to vote when universal male suffrage was introduced in 1917, but the King retained extensive powers and little initially seemed to change. Elections in September 1919, however, brought a majority for the new Peasant Party and the National Party, based in Transylvania and an area recently acquired from Hungary. The government they formed was soon dismissed by the King. In January 1922 the long-established Liberal Party under Ionel Bratianu returned to power and remained in office, with the support of the

King, for most of the time until 1928. In 1927 King Ferdinand died and a regent was appointed.

Ferdinand's son, Carol, had already been sent into exile following official displeasure at his liaison with a particular mistress — although his unacceptable political views were the more likely cause of departure. In November of that year Bratianu also died and the Liberals fell into disarray. In 1928 the National Peasant Party (established by the former coalition partners of 1919) won a major victory under Iuliu Maniu and proceeded to enact a set of democratic reforms and measures to open up the economy. National Peasant leaders, however, fell prey to the temptations of the corruption well established in Romanian public life and Maniu was further embarrassed by the return of King Carol, who continued to refuse to get rid of his mistress. Maniu resigned on this issue in 1930 and the National Government fell, opening the way for the King to restore a monarchical form of rule. This political role he maintained until 1938 in accordance with the extensive powers granted him under the constitution.

The Baltic states

Liberal democracy generally fared little better in the northern reaches of Eastern Europe. All three Baltic states were small, with Lithuania having the largest population at just over two and a half million. The Baltic states had no history of independent modern statehood and owed their independence to the joint defeat of Russia and Germany in the world war. But although beaten and in political disarray, the defeated imperial powers were still intimidating neighbours. It was not surprising, therefore, that questions of security were a major preoccupation in the Baltic states and that strong, dictatorial regimes with close relations to the military were often favoured. This tendency did not fit well with the democratic constitutions initially adopted and the strongly proportional form of representation they provided for. Lithuania also had the unco-operative attitude of Poland to contend with and fell prey to Piłsudski's determined policy of creating an extensive multinational Polish commonwealth, thus losing its historic capital, Vilnius. This strengthened the strongly critical attitude of the Lithuanian right towards the left-wing government for granting too many concessions to national minorities and being insufficiently strict with communists in general and the Soviet Union in particular. Against this background the Lithuanian government was overthrown in December 1926 in a military *coup*, and a number of leading politicians were arrested.

Political instability was rife in Estonia, and 20 different governments held office between 1920 and 1934, with a communist rising also breaking out in 1924. Although not particularly successful in establishing conditions for a stable democracy, the new constitutional order, nevertheless, survived until later moves to establish a more powerful executive emerged in the 1930s. Latvia, too, saw extensive government instability throughout the 1920s but the constitutional system survived the decade there as well. Small parties proliferated on the basis of very lenient requirements for parliamentary candidates, and the situation of semi-permanent crisis dispelled most hopes of effective parliamentary government. It was not, however, until 1933 that steps were taken against the growing threat of radical right-wing forces, with parliamentary government being suspended the following year.

Finland

Somewhat more distant from the critical areas of post-1918 Eastern Europe, Finland had greater success in maintaining democratic structures and processes. Finns belonged more to the Scandinavian world – having been subjects of the Swedish monarch until the early nineteenth century – than to the contested zone that lay between Germany and Russia. But, like Poland and the Baltic states, it owed its full national independence after 1918 to the collapse of Russian power. It also shared much of the experience of the rest of Eastern Europe, as the strength of German power was felt throughout practically the whole of Europe from the early 1930s. Although Finnish nationalism came to be extremely anti-Russian in tone, the country also developed a strong Social Democrat Party. It contained some highly radical currents and forged powerful links with equivalent Russian forces, particularly the Bolsheviks.

In Finland it was right-wing forces that won the civil war which broke out in 1917 following the revolution in Russia. They were by no means content with the conclusion reached at the end of the conflict which, it was felt, gave Russia too much territory in Eastern Karelia. Tensions were further strengthened in 1918 with a split in the Social Democratic Party. Its radical wing established itself as the Finnish Communist Party in the adjoining Russian area of what was now called the Soviet autonomous region of Karelia. This discredited the remaining Finnish socialists and helped exclude them from power, making the formation and maintenance of democratic governments a very difficult process. Democracy was, nevertheless, maintained throughout the 1920s and it was not until 1932 that stronger tensions between left and right developed.

The democratic record

Of the major countries of Eastern Europe, then, it was only Czechoslovakia that maintained an effective democracy throughout the 1920s. The record elsewhere was less successful:

- Never solidly established, the new Polish democracy was badly shaken by the *coup* of 1926. Even fewer political freedoms were in evidence after the elections of 1928.

- Hungarian democracy hardly got off the ground following the turmoil of the closing stages of the war and the formation of the Soviet Republic soon afterwards. Although based on some kind of electoral mandate, Horthy's rule from 1920 was solidly authoritarian and fully subject to the interests of the conservative establishment.
- Political democracy made even less progress in the Balkans. No semblance of democracy or signs of modern government ever appeared in Albania.
- Prospects for the development parliamentary democracy disappeared in Bulgaria with the overthrow of Stamboliiski in 1923, although democratic initiatives like that which saw the electoral victory of the People's Bloc in 1931 were still possible prior to the further *coup* of 1934.
- Romania saw even fewer signs of effective democratic practice, but here, too, electoral victories like those of the Peasant and National Parties in 1919 and 1928 temporarily opened up the possibility of some kind of democratic alternative to the authoritarian, though largely constitutional rule, of the monarch.
- A tenuous form of democracy also lasted for a few years in Yugoslavia, but was clearly doomed by the parliamentary murders of 1928.

On the margins of Eastern Europe, democracy was more secure throughout the 1920s in Finland and more or less survived in Estonia and Latvia, as it did (under growing pressure from increasing polarised right and left forces) in Austria. Only to a limited extent, then, were the major ideological challenges of Communism and Fascism involved in the disappearance of prospects for liberal democracy in Eastern Europe during the 1920s. In most cases the early problems of establishing a democratic system were never surmounted. Traditions of violent conflict and profound social divisions in some countries gave it virtually no chance of taking root at all.

Apart from the establishment and consolidation of political democracy — an area in which they were not notably successful — the leaders of the new East European states shared several other broad objectives. One major priority was the enactment of land reform and transfer of land from the minority of traditional large landowners to the mass of peasants and agricultural workers. A second important goal, closely linked with the first, was industrialisation and the replication of the generally successful patterns of economic growth achieved in Western Europe. A third pressing concern was the achievement of a security framework that would help maintain the survival of the new states. This generally involved the formation of a system of alliances that would support mutual security and keep threats to the peace of the region at bay. In all three respects, the balance of achievement in the early years of the new states was a mixed one.

Land reform

Some measures of land reform were enacted but, where most needed, the level of achievement was only limited. Bulgaria was already well advanced in ensuring that the land was divided out equally. But, as in other countries of the region, this did not do much to improve living conditions for the agricultural population. In the poorer, more backward countries much of the agricultural population was surplus in the sense that the same level of production could have been achieved without it (see Table, below). Rural poverty was widespread and exacerbated by falling prices; Bulgaria's peasantry was afflicted by increasing indebtedness and there were natural disasters at the beginning of the century — all conditions that encouraged the formation of Stamboliiski's Agrarian Union. Once in power the agrarian leader proceeded to limit land-holdings to a maximum of 30 hectares for all families, with a slightly higher allowance for those with more members. After Stamboliiski's murder the policy of land distribution was continued by his successors. By the end of the 1920s about 100,000 peasants had benefited from the land fund established by the government.

Condition of the agricultural population in Eastern Europe			
	Population dependent on on agriculture (%)	Estimated surplus population (%)	Productivity: units per sown area
Albania	80	78	17
Yugoslavia	76	62	17
Bulgaria	75	53	19
Romania	72	51	17
Lithuania	70	27	17
Poland	60	51	18
Finland	57		22
Estonia	56	0.4	17
Latvia	55	—	19
Hungary	51	22	21
Greece	46	50	18
Czechoslovakia	33	—	31
Austria	26		37
France	29		26
England/Wales	05		46

In neighbouring Romania the situation was quite different and, while in 1905 95 per cent of farm plots were smaller than 10 hectares, nearly half of all arable land was occupied by 5,000 or so large estates. The growing

44

commercialisation of agriculture and greater dependence on grain exports in the early years of the century only widened the extremes of rural inequality. Such changes helped create the conditions that gave rise to the violent peasant revolt of 1907. Some kind of reform was unavoidable and, after the war, a general ceiling of 100 hectares was placed on land holdings and 6 million hectares were expropriated. Forty per cent of arable land was eventually redistributed, but peasants did not have the capital or training needed to make real improvements in their situation. Rising population, too, soon increased the pressure on land resources once more.

Yugoslavia had remained one of the most agricultural countries in Europe, but less land was distributed there than in Romania. Two million hectares was affected, about a quarter of the total area overall. Outside central Serbia this did little to help the fundamental problem, while population pressure on scarce resources never slackened. In 1931 over two-thirds of Yugoslav peasants still had less than ten hectares. About the same proportion of land was redistributed in Poland and, while agriculture in the former German areas was quite efficient and well capitalised, the situation was quite different in the old Russian and Austrian territories where overpopulation was also a major problem. Only minor changes in terms of land distribution were made in Hungary, where neither the leadership of the Soviet Republic nor the subsequent conservative oligarchy showed much sympathy for reform along the lines that the mass of peasants favoured. Little effort was made to push forward the implementation of the already modest land reform of 1921, although in the case of Hungary a low rural birth-rate and relatively high agricultural prices during the 1920s meant that the material situation of the countryside was, in relative terms, not particularly severe.

Even in relatively prosperous Czechoslovakia there was considerable land hunger amongst the peasantry, both Czech and Slovak. Property limits were less stringent than in Bulgaria and Romania, and legislation was passed to expropriate land only from large estates of over 150 hectares (250 hectares where they were composed of forest). Such measures reflected the relatively powerful position of the country's richer peasant farmers, particularly in Czech areas where they were well organised. The reforms were also targeted at existing Hungarian and German landowners, whose position was correspondingly weakened, but only at the cost of further stoking the embers of German resentment. At best, the advantages gained from land reform throughout Eastern Europe were limited — and they were particularly meagre where the need was most pressing. A further challenge was to emerge at the end of the 1920s with the onset of international Depression. This was to confront the countryside with catastrophic problems which had dire consequences both economic and — ultimately — political in character.

● **Land reform**

Economic development

The second objective for post-1918 Eastern Europe was stabilisation and consolidation in terms of the basic patterns of production, consumption and trade. Governments attempted to initiate processes of economic growth which would enable Eastern countries to catch up or at least follow the path mapped out by the more advanced West. The extent of war-time destruction and the economic devastation it involved was one problem. But another fundamental difficulty facing the whole region was the wholesale disruption of existing networks of production and trade, as well as much of the regional transport infrastructure, by the collapse of the former empires and the parcelling out of their assets to the large number of new and far smaller states.

The general dislocation affected individual states in different ways. The major pre-war capital market which centred on Vienna was largely destroyed, and Austrian prospects were further chilled by the reluctance of the new Czechoslovak state to supply the country with coal. Poland was endowed with three separate railway systems running on different tracks with incompatible gauges. The modern state was also composed of areas inhabited by Poles that had not been under the same ruler since the eighteenth century. This put formidable obstacles in the way of the country's integrated economic development. Less than 10 per cent of the country's trade had been conducted before the war between the three parts of Poland controlled by the different empires. Former owners were, not unsurprisingly, unwilling to relinquish their former property rights, and the persistence of conflicting claims over economic assets accompanied national tensions as major stumbling blocks in the development of co-operative interstate relations. A number of such general problems affected the region, although the governments of the new states were able in some cases to work out individual policies to deal with them. Successful economic development often depended on how well the national policies worked and the extent to which individual countries coped with the general problems of backwardness and regional fragmentation.

In Czechoslovakia, by some way the most developed country in the region, a financial reform in early 1919 established a solid basis for further progress at an early stage when the depreciated Austrian crown was replaced by a new Czechoslovak currency. With this constructive start the economy functioned well in the 1920s. Czechoslovakia escaped the inflation that hit other East European countries, and this fundamental obstacle to coherent economic development — together with the highly threatening political problems it provoked elsewhere — was successfully taken off the agenda. The problem was certainly not avoided in Poland. Inflation went through the roof in 1923, when a US dollar was worth 2.3 million Polish marks — compared with just 9.8 marks in December 1918. Problems of national economic integration were also particularly pronounced in Poland, with isolated areas of development like the metallurgical and coal-mining centres of the Dąbrowa basin and the textile plants of Łódź being concentrated, respectively, in Upper Silesia and parts of the former Congress Kingdom. Such industrial centres only made economic sense, initially at least, in terms of their relations with the now distant markets of the former imperial powers of Germany and Russia. Transport and other forms of infrastructure in Poland were also sharply disrupted on the lines of the former partition — on top of the enormous losses caused by war-time destruction. The country's industrial recovery and production growth were, therefore, rather more limited than in most other countries.

Contrasts in economic strategy

One approach to economic development was typified by Romania. The conservative patterns of centralised development seen in the cautious path of political change taken in the country were replicated in the economic sphere. Under Bratianu the Liberals were committed to the relatively progressive view that industrialisation was necessary for economic development if national poverty was to be overcome and Romania play a more prominent role on the international scene. In view of the considerable gains it made from a limited participation in the war effort and the relative weight it now exerted within Eastern Europe, Romania's position was not an unfavourable one. But on virtually all counts the country was very backward in the 1920s and hardly helped by the lingering Ottoman traditions of extensive corruption and bureaucracy. Foreign capital was regarded with great suspicion and the political influence that foreign contact might bring still feared. This meant that agriculture and the peasantry were regarded as the main source of development funds, as they had been before the war. The dangers of such an approach had been fully demonstrated by the parlous condition of the peasantry in the early years of the century and the uprising this had caused in 1907. Significant attempts at land reform just after the war meant that rural conditions had changed to some extent, so that the route of independent national economic development did not have to be followed quite so blindly. Industrial production did, indeed, rise significantly after a pronounced drop in the war, but this could still only be achieved under the policy adopted at the cost of a decline in the standard of living for the peasantry and was accompanied by serious currency instability.

Economic policy in Hungary took a quite different turn. Count Bethlen, who took charge as prime minister in April 1921, saw that the lack of domestic resources for effective economic consolidation and development in the recently truncated country needed foreign finance and an openness to help from abroad. Like most other countries, Hungary was hit by massive inflation in the early post-war years and a substantial foreign loan was obtained in March 1924 to help tackle the problem. The assistance was intimately related to other considerations of foreign policy, particularly Hungary's accommodation to the post-war settlement embodied in the Trianon treaty. This meant its acceptance of the painful imposition of a minimal Hungarian state, as indeed happened in the similar cases of Austria and Germany. It also directed Hungary's conservative government to pay attention to the country's indigenous assets, including the substantial Jewish population and the major economic resources they controlled. A constructive approach in this area distinguished Bethlen and the Horthy regime from the right-radicals whose influence had grown after the short-lived Soviet Republic of 1919. On this basis, industrial development proceeded quite satisfactorily throughout the 1920s, and levels of foreign trade grew rapidly.

In Yugoslavia industrial growth was more slow. It continued to provide only limited employment opportunities for the extensive, and still growing, agricultural population. Nevertheless, progress was made, with assistance from German war reparations, and industrial production grew on protected national ground behind substantial tariffs. Protectionist policies were widely followed throughout the region (although no other country took economic nationalism to the level seen in Romania), and this provided a solid base for development throughout the 1920s as the international economy in general worked to make good the destruction caused by the war and a climate favourable to steady growth prevailed. Smaller states had to take particular care to position themselves in relation to changing patterns of commerce and international trade, a manoeuvre achieved quite successfully by the Baltic states which helped to mitigate the effects of some of their political problems. Problems of state formation, the creation of a unified framework for economic activity and the legacy of war-time and post-war dislocation all exercised a critical influence on the prospects for economic recovery and development of the different countries. The challenges were different for each country, and various solutions were adopted. It was not necessarily in the newly created states that such problems were most pressing, and one of the most difficult economic situations was that of Greece, then burdened with a massive influx of refugees from the newly constituted Turkish territories.

The international context

Patterns of economic development and industrial growth were reasonably steady throughout the region once the initial problems were tackled. Initial territorial consolidation took some effort, governments had to marshal depleted and dispersed resources within new national boundaries and deal with the dire threats of inflation and currency instability. Measures were also taken to tackle rural poverty and provide a sounder basis for agricultural production. In several cases it was, indeed, the farm sector that was decisive for the national economy overall and general economic stability. But achievement in terms of economic development was hardly spectacular. Rates of growth were generally lower than those experienced before the war, and development during the 1920s even in the advanced Western countries was fuelled more by speculation and financial ventures than by the technological breakthroughs and production innovations that had boosted the dynamic growth waves of the nineteenth century. This also meant that only limited assistance was provided for the process of development in Eastern Europe.

The world-wide Depression that followed the financial collapse in the United States during 1929 dealt the puny economies of the new states a body blow that critically affected their prospects of development (see page 57). It dramatically demonstrated the significance of the external context for East European developments overall. Trade and foreign links were by no means neglected during the 1920s, but it was only at the end of the first decade of independence that the critical importance of the international environment for East European economic development fully emerged. The fact was that any idea of national independence in this area was largely illusory. The main economic condition for the emergence of a new Eastern Europe was the exchange of an Austrian and German (and — in the case of Poland — largely Russian) dominance for one deriving from Western Europe and the United States. Thus, control of the two largest Czechoslovak firms passed from Austria to Britain and France. Polish capital was 60 per cent foreign in origin in 1928, and Hungarian 50 per cent. Balkan industry was often even more dependent on foreign finance. The role of the international context and the impact of neighbouring powers was equally dominant in security matters and the capacity of the new states to safeguard their independence. In this sphere it was to be the 1930s that was to be the decisive decade. But questions of security and the formation of new alliances to support the position of the vulnerable new states were a major focus of attention from the outset.

The issue of security

The pursuit of national security was the third main objective of the new governments. At the time of the peace negotiations in 1919 and the years immediately following the situation looked relatively promising — although peace was yet to be fully established throughout the region and hostilities between East Europeans themselves had by no means run their course. The influence and military capacity of the former Central Powers seemed to have been successfully curtailed. Austria and Hungary had been separated and their territories much reduced, while the closing phase of the short-lived Soviet republic in Hungary already showed that country's vulnerability to Romanian influence. Germany was less reduced in size but, for the time being at least, its power appeared to be strictly controlled by economic reparations and military restrictions. In terms of the great power farther East, Russia, too, was radically weakened by revolution, civil war and foreign intervention and was, in 1920, defeated militarily by one of the East European states themselves, a resurgent Poland under Marshal Piłsudski.

The establishment of a new forum to help resolve future conflicts and advance the cause of international peace was also agreed at Versailles (see Chapter 3). The League of Nations was established there and provided some hope for continuing peace and the preservation of international order. But other developments pointed from the outset to the emergence of security problems in the relatively near future. America, whose involvement in the recent European war had helped turn the tide for the Allies, soon lost its interest in political developments in the old Continent and refused any further commitment. Its concern for economic matters was less limited, and economic opportunities continued to be seized when they presented themselves. But the US Congress did not ratify the Treaty of Versailles under whose provisions the League of Nations was set up, and America never became a member. Confidence in the capacity of the newly established League to live up to the expectations that had attended its formation was therefore generally limited, particularly in light not just of the US refusal to join the organisation but also because of the absence of other major states from its deliberations.

It was not just the United States that had little interest in the establishment of security in Eastern Europe. Amongst the major powers Britain, too, had no historical and strategic interest in Eastern Europe. It returned to focus its attention on domestic affairs and the country's position within a broader trading sphere, particularly its empire whose territorial extent reached its peak during the inter-war years. The Anglo-Saxon allies generally kept their distance from Eastern Europe and did not greatly seek to influence developments in the region. Much of the weight of European security thus seemed to fall on France, which was severely weakened and considerably exhausted by the war (many of whose critical battles had been fought on its soil). France was, too, by no means a dominant power and possessed a limited capacity as well as a doubtful commitment to coping with the series of challenges to international order and regional security that soon began to emerge in Eastern Europe.

Regional security arrangements

Steps were taken by some states to enhance their own security within the region themselves, although their vision was often limited. A dominant concern in early initiatives was the power structure of the former era and fear of Hungarian attempts to restore some its former influence. Czechoslovakia, Romania and Yugoslavia thus formed a Little Entente during 1920 and 1921. Individual countries subsequently made treaties with

France to help safeguard against external aggression. Such arrangements were clearly limited and did not promise any high level of regional security, although it was hardly possible in the early 1920s to foresee the level of aggression that would be unleashed against some of the East European states towards the end of the following decade. Poland, for one thing, was excluded from these regional agreements as they were largely concerned with the threat of Hungarian revisionism which did not give it any cause for concern. Polish-Czechoslovak relations, moreover, were never very good — as was generally the case between immediate neighbours. In this area, particular tensions were present over the Teschen area. Poland remained dissatisfied with the decision of the Allies, taken at the height of the Polish-Soviet war, to leave a small though significant Polish minority in

The view of Locarno in Pravda. *The British Foreign Secretary, Sir Austen Chamberlain, sets his pawns, Poland, Czechoslovakia, France and Germany, against the more powerful Soviet piece which looks on with contempt*

● **Regional security arrangements**

this region within the borders of Czechoslovakia.

Neither was the general climate of international opinion helpful to the establishment of an effective security order. East European governments were often not convinced either of the legitimacy of other states in the region or of their capacity to survive. Confidence in future stability was shaken when relations between the former main enemies began to be restored. The Locarno Treaties were signed in 1925 and Germany was allowed to enter the League of Nations. Some of their implications were indeed ambiguous. London was willing to confirm Germany's western border with France but not that which had emerged in the East on the Polish border. This did not encourage confidence in the security of the existing East European state system. It also reflected a fundamental divergence between the views of France and Britain in this respect. Major sectors of German society, too, had never accepted the full extent of the country's defeat and the elimination of its imperial aspirations. Former territories continued to be regarded as temporary losses, and the massive economic reparations were much resented. The prevalence of such views led a major figure like Czechoslovak foreign minister Edward Beneš to doubt whether German power was containable within the region and any degree of lasting security could be established under these conditions.

The prospects of international stability and East European security were therefore quite limited from the very beginning. It was not, however, until after the overall weakness of the region had been exposed with the onset of the Depression and when the resurgence of German power really got going under Nazi leadership that the lack of security guarantees for the East European states made themselves painfully evident (see page 59). By this stage, too, the practices of liberal democracy had been gravely weakened or eliminated in all major East European countries apart from Czechoslovakia. Most countries had seen the disappearance of any hopes of establishing a reasonably democratic system. This was associated with the rise of radical right-wing forces. They made the spread of German influence that much easier by exacerbating internal domestic conflict and producing some admirers of the German dictatorial model.

Why was Czechoslovakia different ?

But one exception existed to the general weakness of democracy throughout Eastern Europe. There is no simple explanation for Czechoslovakia's success in satisfactorily establishing and preserving its democracy. It is surely not irrelevant that the country as a whole was more developed and better off materially than any other in the region. While economic wealth does not lead directly to tolerance, civic freedom or the establishment of democracy, it certainly helps by promoting literacy and the emergence of an educated public. This, in turn, creates the conditions for effective social organisation and broader patterns of political participation. While social inequality is not always reduced by national wealth — although it often is — it does reduce the extremes of poverty and deprivation, moderates feelings of frustration and weakens some of the sources of social frustration. Material sufficiency at least provided the basis for a modern democratic form of politics barely conceivable in countries throughout the Balkans.

But in any case Czechoslovakia also lacked the fundamental tensions and divisions that were embedded in some of the new states from the outset. Examples elsewhere included the passionate Serbian nationalism that clashed with an equally strong Croat identity in the Yugoslav state, sentiments of aggrieved Hungarian nationalism and the revisionist quest present from the inception of the post-1918 state, and the profound gulf between the Piłsudskiite and Dmowski camps (in association with a plethora of other political, national and social divisions) in Poland. Associated with the relative wealth of the country and the absence of aggressive political attitudes were the more co-operative attitudes shown by most political forces and their leaders — at least in the Czechoslovakia of the 1920s — and the political skills they were able to deploy. There was both a general willingness and capacity shown by political parties and organisations, generally shared by the groups they represented, to bridge social and political divisions for the benefit of the community as a whole. This attitude was not generally present elsewhere.

Politics throughout much of post-First World War Eastern Europe was seen more as a life or death contest and victory invariably meant the defeat — and possible annihilation — of the opponent. Some historians have therefore laid the blame for the failure of democracy in most East European countries during the 1920s explicitly on internal factors, and on the failure of the governments of the newly established states to cope with the problems that faced them. This mostly happened, after all, before the impact of international Depression and the rise of the German Nazis. These developments were, indeed, to have a profound effect not just on the remnants of East European democracy but also on the independence of the region's new states. By the time Hitler's policies came to dominate the region there were few countries that could boast much in the way of healthy democratic practice. But other interpretations lay more stress on external factors and agree that, while domestic arrangements and social conditions in Eastern Europe were hardly favourable for the development of liberal democracy, this was not the whole story.

Domestic and international influences

Elements of internal and external causation in the origins and development of the post-First World War Eastern Europe were so intertwined that any attempt to draw a watertight distinction between the two is largely beside the point. Domestic conditions might have encouraged the development of democracy and its relative consolidation in Czechoslovakia during the

1920s, but they were to count for little in 1938 when Nazi Germany marched in and destroyed both democracy and the independent republic (see page 63). In fact, when it came to final outcomes, it seemed to be the international context that really counted throughout the region. The major external factor influencing the development of Eastern Europe, of course, was the outcome of the First World War. Before 1914, equally, it was the situation and attitudes of the great powers and continental empires that determined the fate of the smaller nations of Eastern Europe. While the particular dynamics of Serbian-Bosnian nationalism played a singular part in lighting the fuse for the actual explosion, and other forms of nationalism existed throughout the region, the broad framework of competition between different nations, states and empires had been in place for centuries and early twentieth-century conditions only provided the context in which new passions and antagonisms could emerge. The East European nations and diverse ethnic groups also had some clout in negotiations with the Allies during the war in terms of lending their support for the war effort in return for promises of post-war autonomy and independence. But it was clearly the major Allied powers that called the shots in the eventual post-1918 settlement.

The so-called 'national principle' enunciated by Woodrow Wilson was decisive here, but it was not uniformly or unambiguously applied (and, indeed, neither could it have been) and the Americans withdrew from any European commitment soon after the Versailles settlement was reached. The situation was unstable both nationally and internationally. External influences were far stronger at some times than at others, and the power exercised by the major states varied as their leaders and policies changed. National initiatives could make their own mark when circumstances allowed. The main force shaping the new Eastern Europe, nevertheless, remained the pattern of great power relations. The primary interests of the victors were satisfied by radically cutting back on the territories mostly occupied by Hungarians and Germans (including the Austrians, although in practice they were less affected). This mix of factors affected the East European states in different ways. Romania, in particular, benefited from the uneven application of the national principle, while Poland — largely by its own efforts — came to include a more diverse ethnic population than the Allies had ever envisaged.

The multi-national experiment was generally left to individual states to work out to the best of their ability. It worked far better in Czechoslovakia than in Yugoslavia, where the domestic conditions for democracy were weaker. International influences were, however, closely involved from the outset and they built the stage on which the subsequent East European dramas were played. The powers were fully implicated in the formation of the states that were to provide the context in which otherwise 'domestic' factors were then to interact to produce further social and political outcomes. International economic influences were also of great importance

Domestic and international influences •

from the beginning of Eastern Europe's post-war development. While the impact of the Depression and the rise of the Nazis were clearly to exercise a decisive effect on the Eastern Europe of the 1930s, then, external factors were hardly less important during the previous decade.

Questions to consider

- What was the relation between state and nation in post-war Eastern Europe?
- How did uncertainty over state borders affect the development of Hungary and Poland?
- Why were ethnic tensions more turbulent in Yugoslavia than in Czechoslovakia?
- How did the peasant problem affect Bulgaria and Romania in the 1920s?
- What were the problems of economic development in Eastern Europe?

5 Eastern Europe in the 1930s – The Resurgence of German Power

The pre-eminence of Germany in Europe

As the East European states experienced growing difficulties in coping with the demands of independent statehood, they also found themselves confronted by the demands of resurgent German power. The failure of democracy was at least in part a response to the overwhelming domestic pressures that confronted them as independent states. But the eventual loss of independence and capture by the German war machine was a direct consequence of the weak international position in which they were also placed. The implications of this position became increasingly apparent throughout the 1930s. Post-1918 Europe was unusual in containing only three great powers: Britain, France and Germany. By way of contrast five or six powers, including Austria-Hungary and Russia, had dominated in the nineteenth century as Germany built up its first modern empire. With only three major levers of power in the 1930s it was, therefore, considerably more difficult than it had been to maintain a balanced international system. Prospects for the development of the League of Nations as a means of maintaining stability also languished once the United States lost all interest in any European commitment. In the absence of any effective international organisation only Britain and France were in any position to counter the resurgence of German power. Britain, however, reverted to its pre-war reluctance to enter into any wide-ranging continental commitment. It still had extensive naval resources but lacked any military strength on the European mainland. France was in a better position in this respect. But it was still in a weak state following enormous losses during the war and remained psychologically scarred by the experience.

Germany was defeated but not critically weakened by the experience of the First World War. Its submission was in this sense a deceptive one. Its former ally, Austria-Hungary, lost not only the war but all imperial power and its territorial identity. Turkey also had the losses inflicted prior to the outbreak of pan-European conflict during the Balkan Wars confirmed. Russia was another major casualty and lost both territory and influence over Eastern Europe. The economic reparations imposed on Germany, argued for with special passion by France and agreed at Versailles in 1919, remained largely unpaid. The war had not been fought on German territory, and the country's industry and transport system had largely survived the hostilities. The application of the national principle left Germany in quite a different situation from its former allies in Austria and, particularly, Hungary. It was now the largest country in Europe with the exception of Russia. The favouring of successor countries like Czechoslovakia under the Versailles settlement even left substantial numbers of Germans outside its frontiers as well as a considerably weakened Austria which remained to be drawn back into the broader German orbit. In strategic terms, its position was even strengthened with the elimination of Russia as an immediate neighbour and the addition of a number of weak and — as it turned out — quite vulnerable states to the south and south-east in place of the Habsburg empire. Germany was far from being a spent force in post-First World War Eastern Europe.

The impact of the Depression

The rise to power of Adolf Hitler in 1933 and the demise of the shaky Weimar Republic placed Germany in an even stronger position *vis-á-vis* Eastern Europe. This was initially evident primarily in the economic sphere rather than militarily. The post-war recovery and economic development achieved in Eastern Europe in the 1920s was abruptly halted by the onset of the Depression. This began in October 1929 with the Wall Street crash, when the American economy slumped and a profound crisis of the capitalist world economy ensued. Falling grain prices caused drastic falls on the New York stock exchange, which in turn hit the economies of Eastern Europe as loan capital was swiftly withdrawn. Export income in Eastern Europe overall fell to two-thirds of the level at which it had stood before the crisis struck, and all countries experienced great problems in funding the debts they had incurred. The consequences were also very serious for Germany, whose economic recovery had been strongly dependent on US credits. By 1932 a third of the German work-force was unemployed. In this situation the peak of Nazi electoral popularity was reached, Hitler's party winning a vote of over 37 per cent in the first of two national elections held in 1932. Having been offered the chancellorship by President Hindenburg in January 1933, Hitler proceeded to call snap elections on 5 March. They saw an increased Nazi vote and, with further nationalist support, the securing of an overall parliamentary majority. On this basis, Hitler got the deputies to vote for a handover of all legislative powers and briskly proceeded to the installation of a full totalitarian dictatorship. The East European states were by no means the only new or recast states to abandon democracy during this period.

The installation of a Nazi dictatorship actually permitted Germany to respond more positively to the economic conditions that had been imposed on Eastern Europe with the onset of the Depression. In some ways this was a distinct benefit for Eastern Europe in the short term. Eastern agriculture did not suffer the full blow that Depression would otherwise have delivered in terms of drastic shrinkage of the foreign market for its produce. For one thing, the absence of any political opposition allowed Hitler to override the resistance of farmers' lobbies and permitted eastern agricultural producers to compete on favourable terms in Germany. This gave Germany major political and strategic advantages. French treaties with Hungary, Yugoslavia and Romania had already been divested of much of their economic — and even political substance — when the French farming lobby resisted foreign competition and effectively vetoed such agreements. Similar opposition from the agricultural lobby had prevailed in Germany during 1931 with respect to Hungary and Romania, as governing parties were forced to acknowledge the voting strength of farmers' groups. After 1933, though, the domestic agricultural veto was no longer effective as Hitler had abolished elections. But economic power was not an end in itself for German policy-makers nor, unfortunately, was its pursuit regarded as a sufficiently effective basis for the establishment of political dominance.

The roots of German aggression

The economic strength of Germany was, as it turned out, a decisive step towards military expansion and conquest of the entire region in the overall pursuit of *Lebensraum* (living space) as far as the farthest eastern reaches of Europe. The nature of Hitler's precise objectives in this area was not particularly clear, although it is easy to identify a general set of beliefs — or rather passions — involving pan-German nationalism, the need for *Lebensraum*, rabid anti-communism, anti-Semitism and dislike of the Slavic peoples. His strategy towards Eastern Europe is somewhat easier to pin down. Austria and Czechoslovakia were early targets for Hitler's expansionist policy on account of their predominant or minority German population. Poland and lands farther East were also regarded as objectives for conquest and domination as the idea of *Lebensraum* took hold. Hungary, Romania and other Balkan countries were less important but had at least to be neutralised. The rapid growth of German power during the 1930s could only have been countered by an equivalent strengthening of Russian — now essentially Soviet — influence, but Stalin's policy was initially isolationist. There was, in fact, little to stop Hitler pursuing his aggressive intentions in Eastern Europe.

Demilitarisation of the Rhineland, the area along the River Rhine in Western Germany, had been a requirement of the Versailles Treaty and was confirmed by the Locarno Treaty of 1925 (see page 52). It had important security implications for France, Belgium and the Netherlands, all of which bordered the territory. The last military units of the former Allies had left in 1930, leaving Hitler with no immediate opposition when he decided to move his troops in during March 1936. But his attitude was very cautious and the military had orders to retreat if they were opposed. This did not happen, as the French were facing an election and were deeply divided while Britain (as

The German leader who was to have so great an impact on Eastern Europe

ever) was not willing to act as its direct interests were not felt to be involved. But the action effectively nullified France's alliances with East European countries, as any move to support threatened countries like Czechoslovakia or Poland through military action would now cause a major war and few thought France likely to take such a risk. Defence guarantees were finally offered to Poland by the Western Powers in March 1939. This led to the outbreak of general war in September 1939 when Hitler attempted to extend the so far successful model of territorial aggrandisement farther East.

But the pattern was not just one of military conquest, and nationality issues — never far from the surface in Eastern Europe — also came into play. Ethnic tensions were used to assist in the destruction of national independence and the establishment of a number of subservient puppet states, the first set up being Slovakia established under Jozef Tiso in March 1939. Hitler's initial targets and the zone of early military aggression thus lay in the north of the region: Austria — his homeland and, of course, a country inhabited by fellow German-speakers; Czechoslovakia — which also had a large German minority and was dominated by the Czechs against whom Hitler had a particular animus; and Poland — the legitimacy of whose state many Germans had never accepted. To the south German aims were more measured and — at least in the first instance — its aggressive intentions less in evidence. The drive to secure German regional dominance was clearly prominent, but in these areas the use of military power to secure strategic objectives was more restrained. In the long run German expansion throughout Europe met little opposition. The swelling tide of German power did not escape all resistance but the advance of German forces throughout the European mainland was not checked until the Russian army held them at Stalingrad at the very end of 1942. This marked the final limit of German expansionism.

Austria

When Hitler took power in early 1933 there was little solid guidance to his future actions. The unpredictability of his actions, his fundamental irrationality, and the diffuse character of strategic objectives — combined with the skill and political aptitude with which they were pursued — made it difficult to define the likely nature of initial policy. One telling early action, however, was Germany's rapid withdrawal from the League of Nations, already carried out in October 1933. This confirmed at an early stage Hitler's distaste and contempt for principles of national agreement, as well as suggesting a willingness to go it alone at the international level with a reliance on Germany's own power and its growing national resources. At the same time though — or at least very soon afterwards — tactical caution and a willingness to forge links with potential allies were shown in January 1934 by the conclusion of a non-aggression pact with Poland. Moves of a very different character were made later that year in Austria when local Nazis attempted to seize power in June, killing Chancellor Dollfuss in the process. By this stage the Social Democrats and trade unions had both been banned, and an agreement signed with Rome which effectively confirmed Austria's status as an Italian satellite. The relations of Italy, led by Benito Mussolini since 1922 and very much the *doyen* of European fascism, with the new German leadership were still exploratory at this stage, and the Italian dictatorship spoke out strongly against German influence and in support of Austrian independence.

Italy was, moreover, still committed to the former Allied position on the European order that had been given expression in the Versailles and Locarno Treaties. Its representatives met with those of Britain and France at Stresa to issue a protest when Hitler reintroduced conscription in March 1935 and moved to build up Germany's military forces to a level above that imposed in the Versailles settlement. Once the Rhineland was successfully remilitarised in 1936 with no significant Franco-British response and Italy, too, had opted to fly in the face of the League of Nations by launching a war of colonial conquest in Abyssinia during 1935, the overall European picture was dramatically changed. Italy moved steadily in Germany's direction to create a new international Axis (a term first used in November 1936) while the Western Powers showed themselves to be persistently unwilling and — as German economic and military recovery proceeded apace — increasingly unable to resist Hitler's policy of aggressive expansionism. Austria, where the rise of the Nazi movement had paralleled that in Germany, now had little choice but to sign a treaty with Germany in 1936. Further pressure secured the resignation of Chancellor Schuschnigg in March 1938 and the *Anschluss*, or annexation, of Austria. This move broke the terms of the Versailles agreement and was specifically prohibited by the Treaty of Saint-Germain. It represented a major change in the geopolitical landscape of central Europe and produced an expanded German *Reich*, which overcame (if temporarily) the division of the German nation into two separate states.

Czechoslovakia

Bohemia and Moravia, the western part of Czechoslovakia, had previously appeared as a distinctive projection into German territory. With the annexation of Austria it was now more fully surrounded by hostile Nazi forces. Hitler had a clear nationalist motivation for turning his aggressive attentions towards Czechoslovakia. It contained a large German minority in the Sudetenland who had, after all, not always been particularly well treated by the Prague authorities (see page 37). But by this stage of developments in Eastern Europe — particularly in comparison with the treatment of the Jews in Germany — the position of the German minority could hardly be the cause of much legitimate complaint in terms of their political status and civic rights. Hitler had a strong personal dislike of the Czechs and the 'unnatural' state they had been permitted to form within the framework of the equally detested Versailles Treaty. Like many other Germans in the former Austria-Hungary, he had responded emotionally to the internal realignment of nations during the late nineteenth century reflected in the greater prominence of Budapest and the Hungarian population. He was also affected by the rapid growth in numbers and mobility of the Czech population that accompanied the rising level of industrialisation. Non-Germans now had more opportunities to organise and were seen as a distinct political threat. Many Germans, therefore, felt they were losing out to the Czechs in parts of the pre-war Habsburg empire and such sentiments were only strengthened by the agreements confirmed at Versailles in 1919.

The currents of a virulent anti-Czech German nationalism were flowing well before 1914, then, and the new possibilities for German expansion that presented themselves in the late 1930s brought them right back to the surface. Czechoslovakia might have had considerable success in maintaining its new democracy throughout the 1920s, but it certainly did not escape the economic blight that fell across the region at the end of the decade. Closely linked by virtue of its location with Germany and Austria, the countries most strongly affected by the Depression, Czechoslovakia was also highly vulnerable to the economic downturn. In common with other more developed countries, the decline in industrial output was particularly marked. Production in Austria and Czechoslovakia fell by 40 per cent in the few years that followed the onset of the Depression, in contrast to a fall of 11 per cent in agricultural Romania. Amidst the turbulence elsewhere in Eastern Europe, the government was slow to respond and did not devalue the currency until 1934. Economic difficulties impinged directly on relations between the different nationalities. High grain prices tended to help Czech farmers and penalise workers in Slovakia, where trade relations were also hit by the suspension of the Hungarian-Czechoslovak trade treaty in December 1930. Support for Slovak nationalism increased. The rapidly growing economic burden strengthened resentment against the slow progress made towards the establishment of Slovak autonomy provided for

Czechoslovakia's future. Hitler, having decided to carve up the Czechoslovakian 'pie', whets the appetite of Hungary and Poland for Czechoslovak territory. (San Francisco Chronicle)

in the agreements on which the new state had been based.

The enemy within and without

The German population of Czechoslovakia was also affected, and its position was further worsened by the imposition of strict exchange regulations by Nazi Germany. The rise of the German Nazi movement was much admired by many of the Sudeten Germans. Czech authorities had already banned the wearing of Nazi uniforms in 1931, and some leaders of the Nazi youth movement were charged with plotting against the state. In response the Sudeten Nazis dissolved their organisation in 1933 and the following year formed the Sudeten German National Front, led by Konrad Henlein. In the elections of May 1935 it won 62 per cent of the German vote. The result seriously weakened the position of established regional groups that had looked positively on a joint multi-national future within the Czechoslovak state and favoured co-operation with the Czech leadership. Decentralisation measures were introduced in response to the growing Nazi movement and reforms made to raise the status of the German minority within the Czechoslovak state.

By way of international response, the Czechoslovak government rejected the formation of closer ties with Germany and the kind of agreements already reached with the Nazi-ruled country by Austria and Poland. The government attempted instead to strengthen existing links with France and develop a new understanding with Soviet Russia. But any hope of effective security guarantees from France had largely disappeared with the advance of military forces into the Rhineland in 1936. Czechoslovakia was left effectively isolated and further weakened internally as the Nazi virus spread amongst the large German majority. The implications of Russia's more co-operative international stance remained uncertain and — as subsequent developments soon showed — hardly to be relied on as a basis of support for the independence of any East European state. Hitler, however, had declared his feelings of responsibility for the fate of the whole German people before the annexation of Austria, the success of which operation only encouraged him to seek a repeat performance elsewhere. For Czechoslovakia the process started with the reproduction of Hitler's views in strong and wholly unacceptable nationalist demands from Henlein and the nationalist movement. The seemingly inevitable outcome was the Munich agreement of September 1938 imposed by Britain and France under which Prague ceded the Sudeten area to Germany.

These developments also kicked the revisionist ball into general play as far as Czechoslovak borders were concerned. Conflicts that had been repressed in 1919 or had gradually disappeared below the diplomatic surface now came back to life. An area dominated by the Hungarian minority was handed back to the long-aggrieved neighbour, and Polish troops seized the contested area of Teschen denied it by the Allies in 1919.

The Munich agreement proved to be very short-lived, and Hitler's troops entered Prague in March 1939 to take over what was left of Bohemia and Moravia. Slovakia was left to languish under a docile fascistic leadership. By these actions Hitler raised the level of aggression several notches. There was clearly no ethnic justification for annexing the Czech areas of Bohemia and Moravia nor any real political reason or excuse for the action. By establishing Slovakia as a puppet state he was embarking on a new career of state making. Finally, by involving Hungary and Poland in the dismemberment of Czechoslovakia, he was also breathing new life into the subdued embers of revisionism and complex patterns of nationalism and ethnic resentment that ran throughout Eastern Europe. There were even strong signs that Hitler would have preferred to have gone to war rather than take Czechoslovakia by quasi-peaceful means. The dangers involved in such ventures were not to be impressed on Germany, as a whole, for some years, but the involvement of Poland in particular in the death of Czechoslovakia looked remarkably short-sighted in the light of developments just over the horizon.

Poland

If the formation of the Czechoslovak state had been one major *bœ noire* of the German nationalists during the inter-war period, the restoration of

Hitler and Mussolini, and their Foreign Ministers, after the Munich Agreement success

Poland had been the other. It was, in fact, the Soviet foreign minister, Molotov, who described Poland as the 'bastard of Versailles'. In this he was for once in full agreement with many Germans. Poland contained no clearly defined areas populated by ethnic Germans that Hitler could focus on, but there was the specific issue of the city of Danzig/Gdańsk whose status remained problematic throughout the inter-war period. The 'Polish Corridor', which the country's access to the Baltic coast was called, divided East from West Prussia and left Danzig officially a Free City subject to Polish customs supervision. For much of the inter-war period this arrangement worked reasonably well. The rise of Nazism attracted sympathy and much interest among Poland's German population but provoked no direct political action (neither, and probably more significantly, did Hitler seem inclined to mount any provocation there in the early stages). Hitler seemed to take the non-aggression pact concluded with Poland in 1934 seriously, at least until the more tempting issues of Austria and Czechoslovakia were dealt with. The Polish government also regarded the pact very positively and Foreign Minister Beck believed that Hitler, as an Austrian, would be more interested in expansion towards Austria, Czechoslovakia and, ultimately, the Balkans rather than being inclined to follow traditional Prussian interests in the East and North-East.

Neither was the German minority a major concern for the Poles

A communist view of the Munich agreement, from the British Daily Worker.
Chamberlain is portrayed as having been taken in by Hitler and Mussolini while the French Prime Minister, Daladier, seems less sure he has done what is right

throughout much of the 1930s. The Piłsudski regime, or *Sanacja* ('Cleansing'), was firmly in power from 1930, but only at the cost of having conducted a highly restrictive election that year and continuing to maintain strict control over all sources of opposition. The leadership became increasingly isolated from society as Piłsudski continued to rule with his ageing circle of advisers, the 'Colonels', who were mostly former colleagues and subordinates from the Polish Legion he had commanded during the war. Poland adopted a deflationary policy like Czechoslovakia in response to the Depression and imposed great hardship and impoverishment on much of the population. In the predominantly agricultural countries like Poland, Romania and Bulgaria agricultural incomes fell sharply during the initial years of the crisis, by between 50 and 60 per cent. This provided conditions for the vigorous growth of right-radical and anti-Semitic organisations. Piłsudski's death in May 1935 brought no real change in the political situation and failed to introduce any new dynamic in the economy or society as a whole. No single successor to the Marshal emerged and the ambitions and conflicting views of his former followers tended rather to create a stalemate, albeit one which was

International response to the German war machine. After the occupation of Bohemia and Moravia, contrary to the Munich agreement, the German tank heads towards Poland. It is time for the boot of France, Britain and the USSR to put a stop to it, according to this cartoon comment published in the Star, *London, 22 March 1939*

increasingly repressive and dictatorial in character.

A constitution introduced in 1935 further reduced the power of parliament and increased those of the president and commander-in-chief. A new electoral law imposed more restrictions on political parties and prompted the opposition to boycott elections both in 1935 and 1938. The ruling group in turn became more nationalist and anti-Semitic in outlook and created a Camp of National Unity as its public face (known in Polish as OZON) to replace the previous non-party electoral front. Despite growing evidence of Hitler's aggressive and expansionist intentions, Polish policy continued to emphasise the need for maintaining a position of balance between Germany and Russia. The government maintained the belief that Poland was a major power that could stand up to either of its now reinvigorated neighbours (it hardly seemed to have considered the even more threatening possibility that it might have to confront both at the same time). The sluggish pace of economic development during the 1930s and failure of Poland's leadership, despite its military origins, to modernise and reform the armed forces made this claim less and less convincing. The bluff was soon called. After the destruction of Czechoslovakia Hitler clearly set his sights on Poland and concluded a non-aggression pact with Russia, signed by his foreign minister, Ribbentrop, with newly appointed Soviet representative, Viacheslav Molotov, on 23 August 1939. On 1 September the German invasion of Poland began.

The outbreak of war

This signalled the outbreak of the Second World War as Britain and France, following Germany's destruction of Czechoslovakia, had finally given guarantees of military assistance to Poland and Romania in the case of attack — although there was precious little they could do in the first weeks or even months after war was declared. Britain had no forces on the Continent in any case, and the aggressive capacity of air forces (particularly in their current state) was much exaggerated. French general, Gamelin, promised the Poles some form of military attack across the German border, but regardless of what he actually offered (some accounts report a major offensive, others a minor diversionary attack) the nature of any possible military relief from the West was very limited.

The only real deterrent to German aggression could have come from Soviet Russia, which both Poland and Romania regarded as fundamentally untrustworthy and the Western Powers only slightly less so. Stalin's purges had only just run their course and 80 per cent of the military command had been eliminated, which did little to encourage foreign confidence in Soviet military capacity. Any remaining notions of military security for Eastern Europe from the Russian side were swept away with the signature of the Molotov-Ribbentrop pact. It was all too obviously an act of direct preparation for the German invasion. Even worse from the Polish point of view was the discovery that the pact contained a secret clause which assured the signatories separate spheres of influence in Poland and elsewhere. It was in accordance with this decision that the Red Army also invaded Poland on 17 September and assisted in a destruction of the Polish state reminiscent of the partition of the late eighteenth century.

Finland and the Baltic states

Germany now engaged in a lengthy period of 'phoney war' with France and Britain while all made preparations for the real thing to begin. Russia moved to take advantage of its new agreement with Germany and launched a war against Finland which, like much of Poland, the Tsarist empire had lost as a result of the First World War and revolution. Unlike most other countries in Eastern Europe, Finland was successful in maintaining a parliamentary democracy throughout the 1930s. It followed the model of Sweden, Finland's other major historical influence, in having a government formed after 1936 by an alliance of Agrarians and Social Democrats. As in many other countries, nevertheless, the Depression had promoted the emergence of more extremist politics in the form of a growing communist movement and a strong right-wing organisation, the Lapua movement. The conservatives succeeded in getting more stringent anti-communist laws passed and then split with the radical right, whose popular support soon declined. In November 1939 the Soviet Union demanded military bases and a revision of the border in Karelia which the Finns rejected, leading to a Soviet attack. The Finns resisted fiercely for 15 weeks but were forced to cede territory to the Soviet Union. The Baltic states, assigned to the Soviet sphere of influence by the agreement with Hitler, were also served with demands for bases and had little choice but to sign pacts of mutual assistance in September and October 1939, before Russia turned its full attention to the Finns. After the fall of France, annexation and full incorporation into the Soviet Union followed during September and October 1940.

The Soviet Union, therefore, made a number of gains around its borders as a result of the Molotov-Ribbentrop pact, essentially restoring its control over territories lost during the course of the First World War. But, while significant for the countries of Eastern Europe as well as the pursuit of Russian strategic interests, the Soviet gains could hardly bear comparison with the military conquests and advance of the Germans. By the time of the incorporation of the Baltic states they had defeated France, Belgium, Holland, Denmark and Norway. Hitler's forces had eliminated all opposition on the mainland and swiftly established direct control over much of Western Europe. During the summer of 1940 they were also engaged in the Battle of Britain, defeat in which only prevented a German invasion of Britain itself. In October 1940 Mussolini decided to make a move on his own account and emulate the other expansionist powers by launching an attack on Greece through Albania. This soon got bogged down and German assistance became necessary to maintain the impetus of the Axis advance. But Hitler's initial objectives in the East had now been achieved. A rapidly decreasing area of manoeuvre was left to those European countries, mainly in the Balkans, not yet conquered or otherwise subject to German interests. Their economies were increasingly subject to German control and governments uniformly authoritarian and strongly influenced by right-wing forces. But it was only in Romania that a radical right-wing mass movement akin to the fascist forces seen in central Europe developed. By the late 1930s they had come to play a central part in the country's political life.

Romania

In 1930 the Romanian monarch, Carol, assumed control over national political life after the fall of the National Peasant government and maintained a relatively stable, if corrupt and clique-ridden, form of rule over the country. The Depression encouraged the rise of political extremism in Romania as in other parts of Eastern Europe. Widespread peasant poverty had in any case persisted throughout the 1920s, its roots having hardly been touched by the development policies adopted. The brute facts of Romanian political life and its attendant corruption, accompanied by pervasive nationalist rhetoric, encouraged the emergence of sentiments of radical opposition. Dislike of Russia and fear of its intention to recover the north Romanian territory of Bessarabia prevented the extreme left from gaining much support. The high proportion of non-Romanians (particularly Jews) in the leadership of the communist movement alienated it further from all with nationalist sympathies. Calls for a programme of revolutionary change of a right-wing character thus became particularly prominent. Such calls were answered by the formation of the Iron Guard (or League of the Archangel Michael) led by Corneliu Codreanu. It laid emphasis on peasant interests and called for the radical land reform avoided by successive Romanian governments. Like other right-radical and fascist movements, though, it did not have much of a concrete programme and articulated general beliefs in nationalism, anti-Semitism and suspicion of an alleged conspiracy hiding behind the parliamentary façade.

In similar ways to the Nazis, with whom it aimed to associate itself, the movement promoted Codreanu as its personal leader and aimed to build up a personality cult around him. It struck a chord not just in the countryside but also among established parties and their leaders, who saw a hope of raising their political fortunes by building on some of its appeal and emulating the dynamic record of Nazi Germany. In elections held in November 1937, Maniu and the National Peasant Party thus proclaimed a non-aggression pact with the Iron Guard and succeeded in depriving the incumbent government of its majority. King Carol tried to limit the Guard's influence. His response was to appoint a minority government headed by the leader of the National Christian Party. But its main policy was anti-Semitism and the incitement of pogroms, which led to such vociferous foreign criticism that Carol dismissed his new prime minister, Octavian Goga, in February 1938 and assumed more direct governmental powers himself. This placed him in more direct competition with the Iron Guard and, following outbreaks of political violence, the Guard was banned and Codreanu placed under arrest. In November 1938 Codreanu and 13 of his

In this cartoon from Punch, *February 1941, Hitler, with Hungary and Romania tied in his Balkan web, finds the arrival of Stalin a complication*

partners were shot, supposedly while trying to escape. Further repression of the Iron Guard occurred after one of its members assassinated the prime minister, Armand Calinescu, in September 1939. Carol's actions in suspending the Iron Guard were not received well in Nazi Germany, but for a period he succeeded in balancing a pro-Western orientation with consideration for German interests — although Hitler's *rapprochement* with Stalin caused considerable problems in view of the clear Soviet designs on Bessarabia.

Carol's position moved closer to that of Germany after the fall of France. A totalitarian constitution was adopted and a noted pro-German, Ion Gigurtu, brought into the cabinet. A 'Party of the Nation' was set up to which members of the Iron Guard were admitted. But this did not save him from the inevitable pressures. In June 1940, in keeping with the Molotov-Ribbentrop pact, the Soviet Union recovered Bessarabia and southern Bukovina; in August Romania ceded southern Dobrudja to Bulgaria and northern Transylvania to Hungary. This amounted to the diminution of Romania's area by a third. As on previous occasions in Eastern Europe, the loss of national territory on such a scale led directly to political destabilisation. In September General Antonescu, in association with established politicians like Maniu and Constantin Bratianu, forced Carol's abdication and assumed absolute power as prime minister. He made the leader of the Iron Guard deputy prime minister, brought other members into the cabinet, and enhanced the status of the organisation by making it the only legal political body in the country. When it launched a wide-ranging anti-Semitic pogrom and political assassination campaign in November 1940, though, Antonescu crushed the Guard with the support of the Germans. They had installed troops in the country during October, and were now more interested in maintaining regional stability and keeping Romanian oil flowing to sustain the war effort. Antonescu then proceeded to rule the country as military dictator, and in this guise joined with Nazi Germany on 22 June 1941 in attacking the Soviet Union.

Bulgaria

While the course of developments in other countries might have been different, the sequence of events that brought other Balkan countries into the German war effort or just secured their neutrality was broadly similar. In Bulgaria as in Romania the impact of the Depression evoked a distinctive political response, although in this case the main effect was seen in the parliamentary sphere and operated through a relatively open electoral process. In 1931 a People's Bloc was voted into power which included leftist middle-class parties as well as some agrarian representatives. Positive measures were introduced to help alleviate the effects of the Depression on Bulgaria's largely agricultural economy: peasant debts were reduced and loan periods extended, subsidies were introduced for those producing for the export market and small land-holdings were protected from seizure for debt. But there were also signs of the growing support for extremist groups seen elsewhere — communists gained a majority on Sofia's municipal council in 1932 and former prime minister, Tsankov, now headed a fascist National Social Movement which attracted increasing support. The agrarians began to show signs of an inability to cope with the demands of government. They became politically isolated and increasingly corrupt. Bulgaria's fragile system of parliamentary rule was finally brought to an end in May 1934 by a *coup* led by military officers associated with *Zveno* (meaning 'Link'), a pressure group with anti-royalist inclinations that also harped on the familiar anti-political party theme.

Zveno was founded in 1927 and argued for a nationally orientated public morality, seeking to put politics above party in a version of the *Sanacja* ('Cleansing') launched in Poland with Piłsudski's *coup* of 1926. Its outlook expressed the dismay of its supporters at the ineffectiveness of the People's Bloc government and the behaviour of its members. The group also feared the prospect of growing international isolation and a national policy too closely linked with Italian interests. Bulgaria, for example, had remained outside the Balkan entente formed in February 1934 by Romania, Yugoslavia, Greece and Turkey. The continuing activities of IMRO (the Internal Macedonian Revolutionary Organisation) also threatened to isolate Bulgaria internationally by giving it a reputation for permanently tolerating terrorism. Swift military action was taken to control IMRO, after which relations with Yugoslavia improved considerably. Diplomatic relations were established with the Soviet Union, while the activities of political parties were proscribed and those of trade unions strictly limited. But the system of quasi-military rule was unstable and General Zlatev replaced the premier, Colonel Gheorgiev, in May 1935. Power moved into the hands of those close to King Boris, who struggled to push the army out of politics. The regime had some success in preventing the dominance both of extreme left- and right-wing political tendencies, as the influence of the communists grew under the leadership of Gheorghi Dimitrov and the status of Tsankov's National Movement rose on a level with that of fascist forces elsewhere.

Bulgaria found it difficult to avoid being drawn into the German embrace. For much of the inter-war period the country's interests had coincided with those of Italy, with whom it shared a dislike for Yugoslavia and suspicion of its intentions. But relations with Yugoslavia had gradually improved over time, while the growing power of Germany was increasingly difficult to ignore. By the end of 1938 Germany had become a very significant trading partner and main supplier of equipment to the Bulgarian army. Bulgaria remained the only one of the states defeated during the First World War not to have regained some of its lost lands, which enhanced the attractiveness of closer links with Germany. When the first territorial adjustments were made in the Eastern Balkans in 1940 Bulgaria received the southern Dobrudja from

Romania, and German influence over the country was correspondingly strengthened. Despite the Nazi-Soviet pact of 1939 which recognised special Soviet interests in the Balkans, Hitler was actually becoming suspicious of the intensity with which Stalin was promoting them. With the fall of France and the campaign against Britain now placed to one side, German pressures increased on King Boris during the autumn of 1940 to opt for closer German partnership and resist Soviet moves towards regional domination. Such pressures became irresistible when the right of German military passage to Greece was needed to support Italy, whose invasion of the country had come to grief and required rapid military reinforcement. On 1 March 1941 newly appointed prime minister, Bogdan Filov, signed the tripartite pact to permit the entry of German troops.

Yugoslavia

A turning point for developments in Yugoslavia had also been reached in 1934, when King Alexander was assassinated in Marseilles by a Macedonian who was found to have links both with IMRO and the nationalist Croat Ustaša. Prince Peter, the next in line to the throne, was only 11 and a regency was proclaimed under the former king's cousin, Prince Paul. The domestic repercussions of this act were not in fact overly dramatic. Paul was repulsed by the excesses of Serbian political behaviour and quite sympathetic to the position of the Croats. Under prime minister Stojadinović, appointed after new elections in June 1935, political controls were loosened and considerable

The assassination of King Alexander of Yugoslavia in Marseilles in 1934

efforts made to improve relations with the Croats, although these ultimately bore little fruit. He allowed the Croat Peasant Party to function but showed little interest in reaching political agreement with Vladko Maček, its leader since the murder of Radić. Maček himself increasingly argued that the solution to the Croat problem within the Yugoslav state required the restoration of democracy, and to this end managed to establish an agreement in the autumn of 1937 between the Croat Peasant Party, the Independent Peasant Party (based on the Serb population that had resided within the former Austro-Hungarian empire), and the Radical, Democratic and Agrarian Parties of Serbia itself. Stojadinović, however, was more impressed by the growing success of the fascist regimes and sought ways of replicating some of their political institutions in Yugoslavia until Prince Paul finally dismissed him in February 1939.

The King appointed a new prime minister, Dragiša Cvetković, and made overtures to Maček. He persuaded him to drop his democratic aspirations and sever links with the Serbian opposition. In this context a new province of Croatia was created during August 1939 (see map on page 77) and a central coalition government formed in Belgrade. This did not satisfy all interests in Croatia, let alone those of the Serbs, but it helped hold Yugoslavia together as issues of foreign policy came increasingly to the fore. Germany required Yugoslavia's formal neutrality at the very least for its projected invasion of Greece, and the government had little option but to sign the Anti-Comintern Pact in March 1941. This prompted a pro-British *coup* which replaced both the regent and prime minister, and led straight to the conclusion of a treaty of friendship with the Soviet Union. Such a show of patriotic bravado was wholly unacceptable to the new master of Europe and on 6 April, the day of its signature, German forces invaded and overwhelmed the country militarily by the end of April. Within a matter of weeks, then, both Yugoslavia and Greece fell to the force of German arms while Bulgaria and Romania had succumbed to a combination of political and military pressure. Albania had seen the transformation of strong Italian influence into direct control as the country was occupied by Mussolini's troops in April 1939, just after Hitler's annexation of Bohemia and Moravia. The conquest of Greece thus completed the subjection of the whole of the Balkans to Axis control.

Hungary

Hungary did not lie on the path of the German advance into Greece, and was spared the military aggression and direct intimidation experienced by the southern states. But in other respects it shared some of the experiences both of the vulnerable Balkan states and of the former Central Powers themselves. As in Germany and Austria, feelings of injustice at the post-First World War settlement remained particularly strong. Revisionism and the desire to overturn the Trianon Treaty persisted as a major political current throughout the inter-war period. In line with the experience of most of the region, the onset of the Depression hit the country hard and prompted a rapid growth in German influence. After the crash of 1929 and the rapid decline in world wheat prices Hungary had found it increasingly difficult to find markets for its produce, a situation not helped by the defensive measures taken throughout the region. Suspension of the commercial treaty with Czechoslovakia in 1930 was particularly important for Hungary. Financial stability was drastically shaken by the failure of the Austrian *Creditanstalt* bank in 1931, with which Hungary's economy had been closely linked, and the escalation of the crisis in Germany. For Hungary, like the rest of Eastern Europe, the German economy remained a major pole of attraction. By 1939 Germany was the destination of 50 per cent of Hungary's exports and provided 26 per cent of its imports.

The leadership of the country had been stable during the 1920s. Count Bethlen was appointed prime minister in 1921 and succeeded in subduing the rampant inflation of the early 1920s with a coherent policy of economic stabilisation. But he was only partly successful in promoting a policy of balanced economic development that was not overreliant on agriculture. When the Depression hit Eastern Europe Bethlen was unwilling to face yet another crisis. He stepped down in August 1931 after 11 years of service. Another conservative replaced him as premier for a short period. But the next appointment in September 1932 was Gyula Gömbös, a leading right-radical who had first come to prominence as an army captain active in the counter-revolutionary movement that had confronted the Soviet Republic of 1919. Bethlen's neo-conservatism had reflected the more liberal currents of the latter years of the Austro-Hungarian empire. Under Gömbös elements of nationalism, anti-Semitism and a growing fascism became more prominent. The right-radicals had been a significant political force throughout the 1920s while remaining on the sidelines of national political life. But nationalist currents were strong and had been continually fed by resentment at the Trianon settlement. The reactionary basis of Bethlen's administration also encouraged radical and even revolutionary views amongst young Hungarians. After the recent disasters surrounding the ill-fated initiative of Béla Kun to set up a Hungarian Soviet republic in 1919 (see page 32) they resisted all communist temptations and turned rather to the right of the political spectrum.

Political extremism found many willing adherents. The dismissal of many of those employed in the oversized former imperial bureaucracy provided a ready pool of the politically discontented. This was continually refreshed by the numerous graduates from the country's universities who could not find appropriate employment. It was a further weak point of the conservative, rural-based model of economic development adopted. The near-monopoly of key sectors of trade and industry by Jews (and their strong showing throughout the professions) only helped push many of the unemployed and otherwise towards the radical right. Once in power, however, Gömbös was more inclined to conservatism than to radical policies. Only after a further parliamentary election in March 1936, in which the radical right gained a majority, did he commit himself to the establishment of a fascist regime. Horthy and the conservatives continued to resist this move, and Gömbös died the following October. A yet more radical force on the right was the Arrow Cross led by Ferenc Szálasi, another army officer who had significant support from extremists in the military. It was kept out of government but scored a major electoral victory in 1939. Szálasi, nevertheless, only rose to head the government after German troops occupied the country in March 1944. The premiership in fact stayed in the hands of relatively mainstream conservatives, but the nature of the strategic choices they faced inexorably steered them towards the German camp.

Only in association with Germany could the country's major objectives hope to be met and any revisionist hopes of Hungarian expansion satisfied. The influence of the Nazi model thus began to impress itself on Hungarian society. Certain measures of anti-Semitic legislation were passed in March 1938 (which placed it in a favourable situation to be awarded parts of Slovakian territory later in the year), and more extreme laws were introduced in 1939. In April 1941 German forces were allowed to cross Hungary to invade Yugoslavia — almost literally over the dead body of the Hungarian prime minister, Pál Teleki, who committed suicide in protest. Hungary, like Romania, joined with Germany in declaring war on the Soviet Union in June 1941, although Horthy continued to fight a losing battle against total German domination.

Germany's dominance in 1941

With the subjugation of the Balkans Hitler's domination of Europe was nearly complete. Large areas of the Continent had been absorbed by the German *Reich* or were conquered by it, several fascist puppet states had been set up, and others forced into compliance. Italy was a major — though subordinate — ally. Only a few states, mostly on the periphery of the Continent (Spain, Portugal, Ireland, Sweden and Turkey — as well as Switzerland), remained neutral and beyond direct German control (see map on page 77).

Only Britain was beyond German control, but the struggling nation could do nothing to counter German power on the mainland and remained dependent for survival on precarious sea-borne supplies. It received a large measure of support from America, which remained outside the war in formal terms. There remained Soviet Russia, in ideological and racial terms supposedly a deadly enemy but complicit in the war Germany had launched in 1939 and a beneficiary of it in terms of its advance into Eastern Europe through Poland, Finland, the Baltic states and northern Romania. Many, including Stalin, now thought it inevitable that Hitler would turn on Russia

Territorial Changes 1938-41

Acquisitions by

▨	Germany
▤	USSR
▨	Lithuania
▨	Hungary
▥	Italy
▨	Bulgaria

FINLAND
Helsinki

Leningrad
Stockholm
Tallinn
ESTONIA
Riga
LATVIA
LITHUANIA
Memel
Kaunas
Vilnius
Copenhagen
DENMARK
Danzig
EAST PRUSSIA
Hamburg
Berlin
POLAND
Warsaw
EAST POLAND
GERMANY
SUDETENLAND
Breslau
Prague
CZECHOSLOVAKIA
Cracow
Lvov
Munich
RUTHENIA
BESSARABIA
Vienna
Budapest
NORTH TRANSYLVANIA
HUNGARY
ROMANIA
Zagreb
CROATIA
Bucharest
Belgrade
YUGOSLAVIA
SERBIA
SOUTH DOBRUDJA
KOSOVO
BULGARIA
Sofia
ITALY
Adriatic Sea
ALBANIA
Tirana
GREECE
Aegean Sea
Black Sea
U S S R

0   250
km

● **Germany's dominance in 1941**

too at some stage. His view had previously been different. Before the outbreak of war in 1939 Stalin appeared to think that the war in the West would be a protracted one, as it had been between 1914 and 1918. He expected it to reflect in some way the contradictions of advanced capitalism and impose a joint burden on Germany, France and Britain that would cripple them militarily and exhaust much of their economic power. Only then, in this view, would Soviet forces need to intervene. They would by then be able to defeat both central and Western Powers and secure the overall triumph of communism. France, however (and the British Expeditionary Force for that matter), collapsed under the German hammer as quickly as the Poles. Stalin was now faced with a triumphant Germany rather than one embroiled in continuing European conflict.

It was in recognition of this fact that Stalin moved to seize the Baltic states and Bessarabia. They were incorporated within the Soviet Union immediately after the fall of France, a step already taken with Stalin's major priority, Eastern Poland, at the first opportunity in 1939. Hitler's broad strategic plans also moved forward at a smart pace. He suspended the main thrust against Britain after the initial failure of the attempt to secure superiority in the air. On 18 December 1940 the directive for Operation Barbarossa was issued. This covered preparations for the invasion of Russia and the carrying forward of hostilities to the East. It foresaw the defeat of the Soviet Union even before the end of hostilities with Britain. Victory on this front would not only resolve the military and ideological uncertainties involved in the unnatural coexistence with the Soviet Union, but also assure Hitler's command over Europe as a whole. A further critical consideration was the seizure of Soviet oil reserves and the opening up of access to much-needed material resources beyond Europe's borders in the Middle East and Asia.

Invasion of the Soviet Union

The German invasion was originally scheduled for May 1941. It had been delayed by the need to intervene in the Balkans to revive Italy's stalled attack on Greece. The speed and efficiency with which Germany was able to submit the Balkans to its demands and carry through the Axis invasion of Greece is likely to have given Hitler an exaggerated idea of his military powers. When the blitzkrieg on Russia was unleashed on 22 June 1941 the initial degree of success seemed to justify Hitler's optimism. The advance was swift but, as in the case of Britain, hopes of rapid overall victory were not met. German forces were in the suburbs of Moscow by the end of 1941 but this was not far or fast enough. The advance was, indeed, already slowed at the end of July and did not get properly under way again until October. The blitzkreig concept applied so successfully in Poland and France did not work in Russia. Neither Moscow nor Leningrad (previously and later known as St Petersburg) was to fall to German forces.

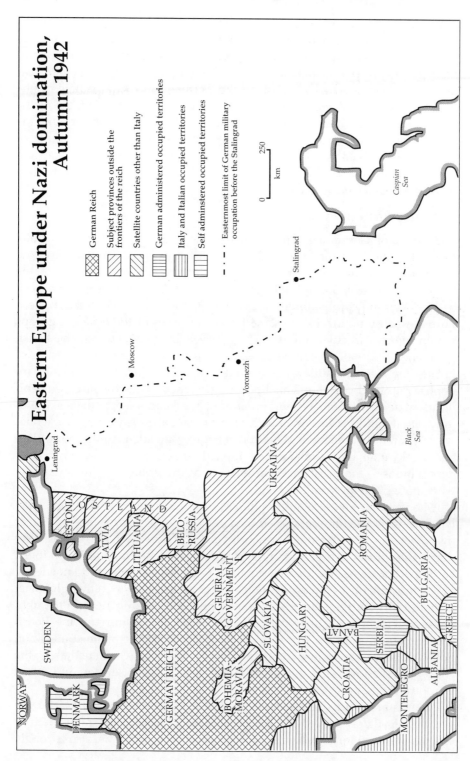

Eastern Europe under Nazi domination, Autumn 1942

Legend:
- German Reich
- Subject provinces outside the frontiers of the reich
- Satellite countries other than Italy
- German administered occupied territories
- Italy and Italian occupied territories
- Self adminstered occupied territories
- Easternmost limit of German military occupation before the Stalingrad

Scale: 0 — 250 km

Caspian Sea

Stalingrad

Voronezh

Moscow

Leningrad

Black Sea

NORWAY

SWEDEN

DENMARK

GERMAN REICH

ESTONIA

OSTLAND

LATVIA

LITHUANIA

BELO RUSSIA

UKRAINA

GENERAL GOVERNMENT

BOHEMIA-MORAVIA

SLOVAKIA

HUNGARY

ROMANIA

BULGARIA

BANAT

SERBIA

CROATIA

MONTENEGRO

ALBANIA

GREECE

● Invasion of the Soviet Union

The Soviet army mounted several counter-attacks and achieved some military successes. But during 1942 the Germans again pushed forward, primarily on the southern front. They thrust well beyond the Aral Sea and made for the Caspian with its copious oil reserves. But by the end of the year and before they reached the Caspian the German advance was held on the banks of the River Volga at the city of Stalingrad (called Tsaritsyn before the habit of abolishing pre-revolutionary names took hold). It was here that the impetus of conquest petered out (see map on page 79). During the course of a lengthy siege held in the depths of a bitter winter, the tide finally changed. Soviet forces encircled and took prisoner a whole German army. From then on the Germans were in retreat.

Occupied Eastern Europe

The extent of Germany's advance up to the end of 1942 had been quite amazing. Hitler's empire extended, in various ways, throughout much of the European Continent. Following the relatively moderate advances of the Soviet Union in 1939 and 1940, the whole of Eastern Europe and well beyond was now fully under the jackboot. But life in occupied Eastern Europe was by no means the same for all countries or the different groups within them. Particular animus was reserved by the Nazis for the Polish population, as well as for other Slavs to the East. After the invasion of Poland the German authorities moved quickly not just to quash military opposition but also to implement policies designed to destroy its culture and incapacitate the nation. Within a matter of weeks this led to the seizure of intellectuals and leading members of professional groups, most of whom were summarily executed. When Soviet forces invaded a little more than two weeks after the Germans they applied similar policies, although mass deportations — no great problem in view of the vast Soviet hinterland — were more frequent from this area.

Amongst the extensive military forces taken prisoner, one major question left open for some time concerned the fate of the officer corps taken prisoner by Soviet forces. After the German invasion of Russia, mass graves were discovered during April 1943 in the region of Smolensk both in Katyń forest and other locations. The discovery tallied with the numbers and knowledge of last movements of the former Polish officer corps in 1939, although Soviet responsibility for the massacre was only fully admitted in 1990. In the light of such evidence, relations between the Soviet leadership and the Polish government-in-exile were broken off. In many ways the Stalinist attack on Polish society was indeed more rigorous and extensive than that of the Nazis, foreshadowing in this way the policies applied elsewhere in Eastern Europe after the war.

Patterns and forms of resistance varied across the region. In Poland the population there proved to be capable and sufficiently motivated to establish a well organised resistance movement that was also strongly independent and drew little support from outside forces. Most other cases of resistance involved to a significant extent the development of communist forces dependent, in one way or another, on the Soviet Union. Poland was an exceptional case in this respect, although a small communist movement did also come into existence. Yugoslavia was the other country that developed a major resistance movement, but one that was sharply split between conservative royalist forces and communists. The division, unlike that seen during the inter-war period, was not so much based on nationality (Croatia under the Germans became a puppet state on the lines of Slovakia) but was no less sharp for that. Hostilities were often directed as much against the other wing of the resistance as against the German occupation forces. Yugoslav communists were also largely independent of the Soviet Union, partly because of communications difficulties in view of the country's distance from Russia and its mountainous terrain.

Opposition took various forms, of which the organisation of internal national movements was only one variant. Resistance to the German occupation of Eastern Europe was not only local but also involved direct co-operation with the Allies. Polish air crew, and to some extent Czechs, played a significant part in the Battle of Britain. Large numbers of Polish troops had been captured in 1939 and sent into captivity in the East after the Soviet invasion of the country two weeks after the incursion of the German army. Sizeable armies were eventually raised from the Poles interned, and they also fought both with the Eastern and the Western Allies.

The Holocaust

Of all the groups that fell under the power of the Nazis the most profoundly affected were the Jews. Hitler was rabidly anti-Semitic from the outset and distinguished from others holding such sentiments by devising a 'final solution' to the so-called Jewish problem which came to mean no less than the complete physical extermination of all Jews who fell under Nazi control. This had particular implications for Eastern Europe and deserves a central part in the region's history for a number of reasons. Firstly, some East European countries had a relatively large Jewish population, which could be traced back to the pogroms and anti-Semitism that had been rife in parts of Western and Central Europe from the Middle Ages. The former Polish Commonwealth in particular had been something of a haven for dispossessed Jews during this period and had consequently built up a sizeable community of those expelled from Western nations. When the Russian empire expanded westward, mostly in the eighteenth century, it was also determined to keep Jews out of central Russian areas and attempted to restrict the Jewish population to its western provinces in a defined 'pale of settlement'. This left Eastern Europe with a relatively high proportion of Jews in the population as whole. Secondly, Jews often tended to occupy an important role in the economy and social structure of some countries (Hungary and Romania, for example). The seizure of economic assets in Eastern Europe by the German conquerors and domestic protégés therefore had a distinctly anti-Semitic aspect.

Thirdly, Eastern Europe was regarded as the most appropriate location for the final solution — not just in terms of the indigenous population but also for Jews from Western and Central Europe. Despite his widely publicised anti-Semitic views, Hitler was strangely secretive about the mechanics of his final solution and was certainly pleased to keep the critical centres of extermination out of the main German areas. For these reasons, the Jews appeared as one of Eastern Europe's major groups in the twentieth century and their fate constituted an important strand in its history. The issues that gave rise to the Holocaust came to the fore in concrete terms as Germany pressed forward during 1941 across former Polish territories into Russia itself. Nazi murder squads were active from the outset and the Jews were amongst those most often targeted. Discussion of the final solution already surfaced in July 1941 and general directives were issued at this time. One possibility initially identified was the relocation of all Jews beyond the Urals, to the East of European Russia, but that variant was taken off the agenda with the slowing down of the German advance. The decision on the eventual form of the extermination programme was taken in January 1942 at a conference on the Wannsee near Berlin. The Nazi concentration camps in Poland, and particularly Auschwitz-Birkenau, were to be expanded and new death camps set up throughout the country. The programme then moved swiftly forward, targeting first the 3 million Jews of occupied Poland and then drawing in the Jewish population of the Balkans, the Low Countries, France and Hungary.

The culmination of the process was reached well after the end of 1942, but it is certainly appropriate to note its outcome in the context of Nazi power rather than that of the Soviet advance examined in the next chapter. The total of deaths amongst the Jewish population under Nazi rule was quite horrendous. A figure of 5.85 million for the overall death toll was presented to the Nuremberg Tribunal organised by the Allies after the end of the war. Such a total is still thought by contemporary historians to be reasonably close to the mark. The enormity of the war crime was not fully recognised during the course of the war itself. There was little the Allies could do to stop or even slow down the process as it proceeded on German-held territory, particularly at the beginning of Hitler's extermination programme. But there was also a disturbing general lack of response to the increasing evidence of its development. Little official account was taken of documents like those produced by the Polish Government in Exile on the fate of the Jewish population, and doubts were expressed by some American authorities (including representatives of the influential American Jewish community) about the credibility of the whole process of extermination. It was only after the Second World War that the full extent of Nazi crimes in this area as well as others throughout Eastern Europe came to be discovered.

Questions to consider

- Why did Germany's position in Europe strengthen so rapidly between the wars?
- How did the German minorities in Eastern Europe help the spread of Nazi power?
- What were the causes and consequences of the Nazi-Soviet Pact of August 1939?
- How did the Balkan countries come under German control?
- What part did the Soviet Union play in the rise and decline of Nazi Germany?

6 Stalin's Victory in Eastern Europe, 1943-1953

The Allied offensive

With the defeat of the German army by Soviet forces at Stalingrad in February 1943, the resurgence of German power that had begun just ten years earlier with the accession of Hitler to the chancellorship was contained. It took more than two years for the Soviet army to drive the Germans out of Eastern Europe, capture Berlin and extend its power as far as the River Elbe — and well beyond its western bank in the north. But the nature of the shift in power that occurred at Stalingrad was clear and decisive. Up till then Eastern Europe — and areas beyond — had increasingly fallen under German influence. From 1943 it was the power of Soviet Russia that reasserted itself throughout the region.

After the Soviet victory the immediate concern and primary objective of all the Allies was to press on to inflict further defeats on the Germans and

German troops captured in North Africa following the opening of the North African front

secure final supremacy over Nazi forces. But as the eastern front was the only one active in the European arena the main burden of hostilities fell on the Soviet forces. Stalin had made much of this imbalance at an early stage and exerted persistent pressure on Britain and the United States to open a second front in Europe. Britain and America had agreed in principle at the second Washington conference (June 1942) that a second front should be opened. But it was a complex and highly difficult operation to mount. The delay in opening a second front in Europe strengthened a general recognition of the primary military role played by the Soviet Union in overcoming the German forces. It gave Stalin a strong moral superiority in dealings with the Western Allies which he adroitly turned to his political advantage. This strengthened his hand in negotiations over the future of Eastern Europe and the extent of the influence that Russia could legitimately expect to exert there during and after the war. A second front was finally opened with Allied landings in North Africa during November 1942. This led to the capitulation of Italian and German forces in May 1943 and subsequent landings in Sicily and southern Italy. But a second front in the key north European area of operations was only achieved with the Allied landings in France on D-Day, 6 June 1944.

The main thrust of the early western attacks on occupied Europe, therefore, lay at some considerable distance from the centres of German power and the heart of the Nazi war machine, whose chief efforts continued

Troops preparing to land in Normandy, D-Day, 6 June 1944

● **The Allied offensive**

to be directed against the Soviet forces. The Western leaders remained acutely aware of this situation and after Stalingrad feared that Hitler might consider making a separate peace in the East. They took great care to mollify Stalin and satisfy Russian interests in as many other ways as possible — which sometimes meant the sacrifice of East European interests and their prospects of post-war independence. This soon became evident in the case of Poland and became increasingly the case with other parts of Eastern Europe. The behaviour of the Allied leaders was in some ways not dissimilar to the attitude of appeasement taken towards Hitler by Britain and France before the war (see also discussion on pages 53-5). The Western Allies — perhaps unfortunately but hardly surprisingly — thus refused to support the Polish position over the Katyń massacre, whose traces were discovered in April 1943, and continued to maintain the view (not just during the war but until the very demise of the Soviet Union in 1991) that no guilt could be unequivocally allocated for the crime. They could contribute little else in the European field of operations as the Soviet army provided by far the greatest force behind the blows that began to drive back Hitler's forces.

The Soviet victory at Stalingrad was followed by a further defeat of German forces in the great tank battle around Kursk during the first half of July 1943. Overall, Soviet supremacy on the eastern front now became apparent and final victory, however hard fought, virtually inevitable. Fighting their way up the Italian peninsular, American and British forces remained at a considerable distance from the critical areas of operation in Eastern Europe, only taking Rome on 4 June 1944. Such was the force and speed of the Soviet advance (particularly in southern Russia and the Ukraine), that the Red Army reached the borders of pre-war Poland on 3 January 1944 and began the liberation of Eastern Europe from Nazi domination well before Western Allied forces had set foot on the Normandy beaches or progressed far beyond the deep south of Italy. As far as Eastern Europe was concerned, however, liberation by the Red Army was by no means an unmixed blessing. The portions of pre-war Poland first freed by the Russians never reverted to Polish control and were integrated with the USSR, with Western agreement, as parts of the Ukrainian and Belorussian Soviet Republics. Early reports had suggested that relations between Soviet forces and the Polish underground were quite co-operative, but a different picture soon emerged.

Ambiguities and contrasts in the Soviet liberation

By the end of July 1944 Soviet military detachments reached the suburbs of the Polish capital on the East bank of the Vistula. Dismayed by the Western handling of the Polish question and apparently faced by the imminent liberation of Warsaw by the Russians, the Polish underground rose against the Germans on 1 August 1944 and fought to restore the freedom of the capital on their own account. The circumstances of the uprising and the precise motives of those concerned remain the subject of continuing debate. While there is some evidence that early Soviet broadcasts in fact encouraged the outbreak of the uprising, the Red Army subsequently sat on the eastern bank of the Vistula as the Polish underground first achieved considerable success with their surprise attack and were then brutally ground down as the Germans reasserted their control. With 200,000 Polish lives lost during the two month long insurrection, the city was then razed to the ground. After the experience of Katyń, the fate of the Warsaw uprising reinforced Polish views that the objectives of Nazis and Soviet communists were by no means dissimilar with regard to Polish interests and, in particular, to that of national independence. There is a strong case for concluding that the Warsaw Uprising of August 1944 was left by Stalin to the mercies of the German army and the SS precisely to weaken domestic Polish forces.

Neither was the fate of Poles in the Warsaw uprising wholly unique in Eastern Europe. A comparable drive for national liberation failed under similar conditions in Slovakia. Plans had been laid by the Czechoslovak émigré government and Soviet groups for armed struggle there, although local guerrillas acted prematurely in late August 1944 and attracted strong German retaliation. Although local conditions again militated against swift Soviet relief, there was also evidence of growing tension between Soviet representatives and those of the émigré government. Whatever the reason for it, Soviet assistance was very slow in coming. There was plenty of time in Slovakia, too, for national liberation forces to be isolated and eliminated before any help could arrive, the process being completed by the end of October under the personal supervision of Heinrich Himmler. In the view of many, the forces of national liberation in Eastern Europe were regarded by Stalin as equally dangerous to future Soviet interests as the resistance of the German enemy itself. But in most areas of Eastern Europe the force of Soviet arms was, in any case, the main factor in liberation from German occupation.

Developments to the south and in the Balkans took a quite different turn, and the national governments there generally had considerably greater freedom of manoeuvre. In Hungary it was only in March 1944 that German troops intervened directly to occupy the country, soon after which Hitler decided to make Budapest the site of major resistance to the advancing Soviet forces by creating a strong southern flank. The fight to defend Budapest was correspondingly fierce and it took Soviet forces seven weeks to take the city, a process that was not completed until the middle of February 1945. The liberation of the Balkans was achieved in the face of considerably less resistance. The Germans no longer had a position to defend. In Romania King Michael organised a *coup* in association with the long illegal democratic parties. After the arrest of Marshal Antonescu on 23 August 1944, a new government was formed under General Sanatescu which ceased hostilities against the Russians and allowed the German troops to withdraw. By the end of the month Soviet forces occupied the oil-fields so coveted by Hitler. Romania now declared war on the former German ally and contributed 27 divisions to the Soviet-led liberation of northern Hungary and Slovakia.

Bulgaria had been loosely engaged in the Axis war effort and did not send troops to fight against the Soviet Union. It was only on 5 September 1944 that the Soviet Union declared war on Bulgaria, which prompted the immediate request for an armistice from the Sofia government. Three days later Bulgaria switched its position completely and declared war on Germany. The following day a pro-Soviet *coup* installed a new government which provided conditions for the Soviet army to complete the occupation of the country without any resistance. Only in Yugoslavia and Albania did local resistance forces play a major part in the liberation, as they did in neighbouring Greece. Belgrade, the Yugoslavian capital, was occupied on 18 October by the communist partisan forces of Josip Broz Tito. They had maintained an anti-Nazi military base throughout the war and had made direct contact with the Red Army just a few week earlier, at the beginning of September. The liberation of Eastern Europe from Nazi domination thus began earlier in the north, was far more fiercely fought and lasted considerably longer as German forces fought tenaciously to defend the German heartland from the Soviet advance.

Great power interests

High-level negotiations between the Allies had been held as soon as the prospect of fighting a joint war against Germany and the other Axis powers came on to the agenda. Meetings between the main national leaders were initially restricted to the Western Allies. The first was held between Winston Churchill and US president, Franklyn Roosevelt, in August 1941, before the formal entry of the United States into the war. It produced an Atlantic Charter which included commitments to national sovereignty and the principle of self-government, international co-operation and the prospect of establishing some general security organisation, and free and equal access of all countries to international resources. It was only two years later, during November 1943, in Teheran that the first meeting of the 'Big Three' (Churchill, Roosevelt and Stalin) took place. The attention of Allied governments was beginning to be concentrated on the nature of the post-war settlement and the form that Eastern Europe was likely to take once the increasingly likely victory over Nazi Germany was finally achieved. By this time Stalin had more than recovered from the shock of the German invasion and the loss of enormous swathes of Soviet territory. Not only had the turning point been reached at Stalingrad but the Red Army had also seen off the last mass German offensive at Kursk. The Soviet leader stood, therefore, in a favourable political and military position with respect to the other Allied leaders. Roosevelt, moreover, was not inclined to discuss territorial changes after the war at all. He was particularly reluctant to pronounce on

Poland as he faced an imminent election and did not want to risk losing any of the Polish-American vote.

The Soviet leader had clear ideas on this subject and did not hesitate to make strong demands to secure his objectives. They reflected a sharp change in the Soviet outlook as it had developed in the early inter-war years. The Soviet Union had been excluded from involvement in the affairs of Eastern Europe for much of the inter-war period, a position that had dire consequences for the Soviet Union as well as the rest of Europe, as the power of Hitlerite Germany grew without any check or effective restraint. Stalin and the Soviet leadership showed little inclination to repeat that mistake in the situation that was developing as the end of the Second World War approached. Their perceptions of the region had recently undergone a major change. The former Russian influence there had largely evaporated with the collapse of the Tsarist empire in 1917, after which the attention of the Soviet authorities became increasingly focused on their domestic base when early hopes of world revolution turned out to be illusory. Once Stalin proclaimed the doctrine of Socialism in One Country in 1926 priority was assigned to the development of social and economic forces within the territory of the Soviet state, and Russian energies where mostly directed to processes of internal development. Both American and Russian policy during the inter-war period thus tended to follow a relatively isolationist current. The fact that both were drawn into a further deadly European conflict little more than 20 years after the ending of the first one prompted both powers to pay more attention to European security concerns as the end of the war approached.

Soviet Russia was firstly committed to regaining territories lost during the revolutionary turmoil after the First World War, an area in which it had made considerable gains in the pact signed with Germany in August 1939. This particularly concerned Poland but also Bessarabia (northern Moldavia) and the Baltic states. Apart from their brief period of independence between 1918 and 1940 the Baltic countries had formed part of the Russian empire since the early eighteenth century. Their incorporation in the Soviet Union in 1940 showed that Stalin was set on re-establishing former imperial borders in this area. Poland posed more of a problem and was now too large and prominent a country to be similarly intimidated into submission. Discussion over its status initially focused on its borders, therefore. Western views after the First World War had not been in great conflict with those of the revolutionary Russian state on this issue. In 1919, for example, the British had proposed the Curzon line (named after the foreign secretary of the time) as Poland's eastern border, which the Poles moved considerably farther East after war with the young Soviet state. The Curzon line roughly divided the area populated almost wholly by ethnic Poles from the eastern marches dominated by a Belorussian or Ukrainian peasantry. It was, in fact, this border that was eventually agreed with Stalin as part of the post-war settlement (it was, too, almost identical with the areas of German and Soviet occupation similarly devised in August 1939).

Russia's historic claim to the eastern portion of pre-war Poland was recognised with little difficulty, therefore, as were the similar demands on the Baltic states and Bessarabia. Poland was to be compensated by extending its western border to take in areas of Prussia and other parts of pre-1939 Germany. The Polish émigré government was, naturally enough, wholly opposed to Soviet seizure of the country's pre-war territory. But after two German invasions of Russia within little more than a quarter of a century it was clear to the Western Powers that the Soviet Union had very legitimate security concerns in this area. It was not regarded as unreasonable that the Soviet Union should also require post-war Poland to install a regime that was 'friendly' to it (although the nature of that 'friendship' and the kind of foreign policy it involved was never specified by the powers). In the event Stalin got what he wanted at Teheran without significant resistance in terms of Poland's post-war borders, as well as securing a firm Western commitment concerning the sensitive issue of the opening of a second front in France.

Agreements between the Allies

The next major meeting between Eastern and Western leaders took place in Moscow during October 1944 and was restricted to Churchill and Stalin. This was the occasion of the renowned 'percentages' agreement reached by the two leaders on the respective spheres of influence of the Soviet Union and Western Powers in post-war south-eastern Europe. The agreement was initiated by Churchill to obtain Soviet agreement on the priority of British interests in post-war Greece. This was the only area in which Britain had any major interest in Eastern Europe in terms of its commitment to maintain a secure route to the Suez Canal — and thus communication and supply lines with its eastern imperial possessions. Stalin, in return, was offered a relatively free hand in Romania, in which a Soviet interest was already well known. This understanding was expressed as a 90 per cent British interest in Greece and a similar Soviet influence in Romania. Precisely what the percentages and influence involved was not made clear, but it seemed to give the major powers a free hand in determining the make-up of governments and shaping policy in those cases. The agreement was extended to other Balkan countries, involving a dominant (75 per cent) Soviet role in Bulgaria and shared Soviet and Western influence over Yugoslavia. A similar 50:50 share in influence was proposed for Hungary, but this also shifted to a more dominant Soviet role by the end of the talks. It did not have any formal status, and precisely how Stalin regarded it was never made clear. But it certainly occupies a prominent position on the historical record and seems to have provided the basis on which the development of the different spheres of influence generally developed after the war.

How this crude version of power politics accorded with the principles of the Atlantic Charter (the declaration of democratic principles agreed by Churchill and Roosevelt in 1941) hardly bears consideration, but the agreement clearly showed that Churchill's only significant concern in this area was for British interests in Greece and that Stalin had every reason to expect a clear run in Romania and Bulgaria, as well as a major basis on which to build Soviet influence in Yugoslavia and Hungary. It was already becoming evident that Yugoslavia was hardly likely — in the initial stages at least — to create a problem in this respect, as it was the one country in which a communist guerrilla movement was mounting fierce resistance to occupying German forces and it showed every sign of intending to forge strong links with the Soviet Union. As a whole, though, the outcome and very process of the agreement implied a major contradiction with developing ideas of a new international community and the principles of the United Nations Declaration signed in April 1942, which also spoke of national independence and the self-determination of peoples. The principles of liberation and independence foreseen by the Allies for the post-war period in Eastern Europe were, therefore, qualified by the needs of the war-time alliance and fudged from the outset, just as the application of criteria of nationality had been in creating the new states of post-First World War Eastern Europe (see Chapter 3). It seemed only reasonable to the Western Powers that due consideration was given to the legitimate security concerns of Soviet Russia following the second conflict with Germany little more than 20 years after the first, as well as to the recognition of regional interests that were similar in character to those of the Western Powers.

Document: Report of the Crimea Conference (Yalta), Declaration on Liberated Europe, 11 February 1945.

The establishment of order in Europe and the rebuilding of national economic life must be achieved by processes which will enable the liberated peoples to destroy the last vestiges of Nazism and Fascism and to create democratic institutions of their own choice. This is a principle of the Atlantic Charter — the right of all peoples to choose the form of government under which they will live — the restoration of sovereign rights and self-government to those peoples who have been forcibly deprived of them by the aggressor nations. To foster the conditions in which the liberated peoples may exercise these rights, the three governments will jointly assist the people in any liberated state or former Axis satellite state in Europe where in their judgment conditions require (1) to establish conditions of internal peace, (2) to carry out emergency measures for the relief of distressed people, (3) to form interim governmental authorities broadly representative of all democratic elements in the population and pledged to the earliest possible establishment through free elections of governments responsive to the will of the people, and (4) to facilitate where necessary the holding of such elections.

A few months later, in February 1945, a second 'Big Three' meeting — and the last to bring Churchill, Roosevelt and Stalin together — was held at Yalta in the Soviet Crimea. Much of the agreement reached there was based on decisions already effectively taken and, particularly, on the facts of the military situation that now prevailed in Europe. It was made clear at Yalta that Stalin fully recognised the primacy of the rights and demands of the 'Big Three' in relation to smaller powers. He articulated further his refusal to compromise any major Soviet interests in relation to Poland and now also spoke strongly in favour of the dismemberment of the German state after its eventual defeat. Stalin had clearly developed a strong conception of Soviet interests and the nature of the post-war demands to be made in this area. This stood in marked contrast to the poor co-ordination of views between the main Western leaders and their failure to develop a clear European strategy for the post-war period.

Friction between the Allied leaders and disagreement over the future shape of Europe became increasingly evident. President Roosevelt was now physically weak and gravely ill (dying only two months later), and was less inclined to contest Stalin's demands than to secure his agreement to the new international organisation that was coming into being as the United Nations. He was most concerned to ensure full Soviet participation in its deliberations and to avoid the fatal weakness that had afflicted the League of Nations, in which the participation of the great powers had been only partial. The agreement at Yalta, while giving Stalin much of which he demanded, still provided certain democratic safeguards for post-war Eastern Europe and foresaw the holding of 'free and unfettered elections' in

Churchill, Roosevelt and Stalin at the Yalta conference

post-war Poland. How the tension between this condition and the agreement that the Soviet Union should have neighbours with an assured 'friendly' foreign policy was to be resolved remained unexplored.

Not long after the Yalta conference a final summit meeting opened in Potsdam, outside Berlin, in July 1945. Roosevelt had been succeeded by vice-president Truman and Churchill was replaced during the meeting itself, having lost the general election to Labour leader, Clement Attlee. Most decisions about Eastern Europe were now fully pre-empted by the disposition of the military forces occupying the region. Truman took a significantly stronger line than Roosevelt had done and complained sharply about the failure of Soviet representatives to apply all parts of the agreement made at Yalta. In the event, though, the question of Poland's western border was still left formally undecided as was the fate of East Prussia, now under Soviet occupation. The latter region was eventually divided between Poland

Stalin, posing as a policeman, helps Russia to burgle Eastern Europe after Yalta. Doubts about the Yalta agreement expressed in the Chicago Sunday Tribune

and the Soviet Union, the Russians taking Königsberg and transforming it into a massive military base, renamed Kaliningrad. To the north of this enclave the independent states of Lithuania, Latvia and Estonia once again reverted to Soviet control (see map on page 95). Finland, however, although defeated by Soviet forces in August 1944, was allowed to retain its independence with the proviso that it maintain a neutral foreign policy and transfer some parts of its territory to Soviet control.

Bases of Soviet dominance in Eastern Europe

The fate of the other East European countries was rather different from that of Finland. Potsdam fully bore out Yugoslav leader Milovan Djilas's report of Stalin's view that, under contemporary conditions, whoever occupies a territory now also imposes on it his own social system. The decisive Soviet role in reversing the German hold over mainland Europe had been quite critical to subsequent developments. General agreement that the Red Army should advance directly on the main front and press forward to the liberation of Berlin as quickly as possible further diminished the prospects for Western influence over developments in Eastern Europe. It was very much the Soviet forces that expelled the Germans from Eastern Europe and, in key areas, they stayed there as an army of occupation. The political role of Soviet representatives and their communist allies in the region was enhanced by earlier German success in destroying all national opposition and smashing all resistance in the early stages of the war. Neither had Britain and the United States been particularly opposed to a major expansion of Soviet influence in this area when the issue was first raised (see pages 86 and 88-90).

Although sympathetic to the idea of Polish independence, then, the Western Powers were in no position to provide the basis for its development. Their view was also a detached one. Britain and the United States did not have any strategic interests in this northern part of Eastern Europe when the topic was first opened for discussion. Their commitment to defend Western Europe from the threat of communism and a clear desire to establish liberal democracy in Eastern Europe was not apparent during the war and the early post-war period. The cold war that dominated world politics in the second half of the twentieth century only tightened its grip some time after the end of the Second World War. New conceptions of great power relations emerged slowly during this period, largely as a result of the continuing development of Allied relations and the growing strains that emerged in the course of the hostilities and the years that followed. But overlying all these considerations was the simple fact that the Western Powers had little choice but to take full account of Soviet interests during the war and the period that followed. Britain and the United States had no real power to counter Soviet actions anyway. Nevertheless, while a dominant Soviet influence was assured by its military presence in Eastern Europe, the precise nature of the post-war settlement still remained to be decided.

Eastern Europe, 1953

FINLAND

Leningrad

SWEDEN

ESTONIA

LATVIA

---- 1939
borders

LITHUANIA

Vilna

Danzig EAST
PRUSSIA

Minsk

Warsaw

U S S R

EAST
GERMANY

P O L A N D

Wroclaw

Cracow

Lvov

Prague

CZECHOSLOVAKIA

Munich

Vienna

Budapest

Yalta

AUSTRIA

HUNGARY

ROMANIA

Trieste

Zagreb

Black Sea

Belgrade

Bucharest

YUGOSLAVIA

BULGARIA

Sofia

Adriatic Sea

ITALY

ALBANIA

Tirana

TURKEY

GREECE

Aegean Sea

● **Bases of Soviet dominance in eastern Europe**

Developments in Hungary and Poland

Amongst the countries of Eastern Europe, free elections were only held in Hungary and Czechoslovakia, in the latter case showing strong popular support for the Communist Party in 1945 and giving it a strong, and quite legitimate, voice in the early post-war government. Far less support was shown for the Communist Party in early Hungarian elections and the Smallholders' Party emerged as a dominant force. Soviet regional dominance, however, meant that eventual communist political victory throughout Eastern Europe was assured. Initial electoral defeat just prompted the Hungarian communists to adopt a different strategy. They established power by using 'salami tactics' to slice away at portions of the political opposition and gradually cut away the power base of all non-communist forces. The Hungarian communists made tactical alliances with the social democrats and majority Smallholders' Party to counteract their political isolation in the country as a whole.

On this basis they strove to reduce the influence of the centre and right wing in the two parties. 'Conspiracies' were discovered which linked prominent figures in the two parties with foreign agents and representatives of the pre-war authoritarian regime. The Soviet occupation forces also played a part and exercised a right of veto over government bills and helped build up security forces, the ministry of the interior having been carefully targeted for communist control. They took the Smallholders' general secretary into custody, and by mid-1947 the prime minister was also implicated in a concocted conspiracy and forced to resign. In elections held in August 1947 under far more restrictive conditions the communists gained 22 per cent of the vote and their allies a further 38 per cent, giving them an overall majority.

Poland and the Soviet zone of occupation in Germany were direct targets for the imposition of strong Soviet control at an even earlier stage. Although excluded from the percentages agreement arrived at by Churchill and Stalin in 1944, there had never been much doubt that the Soviet leader intended to exert just as strong an influence over that country as it did over Romania and would brook no opposition in the process of regaining Poland's eastern territories. A major difference from Romania, however, was that Poland had been an Allied power and was a considerably larger country with a well-established tradition of nationhood whose very existence had been challenged by Russia on more than one occasion. By and large, though, the Allies' tense relations with the émigré government, their refusal to take up the issue of Katyń, and their inclination to agree with Soviet demands for an eastern border of the country broadly in accordance with the Curzon line (see page 89) all tended to imply that the Western Powers were unlikely to mount much resistance to Soviet initiatives in this area.

After it had broken off relations with the government-in-exile over Katyń, the Soviet leadership upgraded the position of the Polish national committee it had established at the beginning of 1943. In July 1944, as the Soviet army moved farther into Polish territory, it was designated the provisional government. As one of the less impressive decisions contained in the Yalta agreement, this provisional government was now endowed with formal status by the Allied Powers. An attempt was made to increase its democratic credentials by ensuring that émigré groups were also given representation on it. Peasant Party leader, Stanisław Mikołajczyk, thus joined the government as deputy prime minister but was unable to exert much influence. No general election was held until January 1947 and a rigged victory for the communist-led 'democratic bloc' was the obvious result.

Romania

In the Balkans the abandonment of Romania to Soviet control had been given a higher level of Western recognition by virtue of Churchill's percentages agreement with Stalin. The Soviet leader indeed kept scrupulously to the condition that he should leave Britain a free hand in Greece. He ordered support and supplies to be cut off from the communist guerrillas there, and stood by as British forces intervened to crush the powerful communist movement in the civil war that had broken out following the withdrawal of the Germans. In Romanian politics the communists were a minor force, as they always had been. By the end of war the party had been banned from public life for more than two decades and had fewer than 1,000 members. But its members were increasingly well represented in the first post-Antonescu governments. Their power was further enhanced in October 1944 by the formation of a broader National Democratic Front which expressed increasingly vociferous opposition to the incumbent Radescu government. On 6 March 1945 Prince Michael was forced to dismiss the premier and appoint Petru Groza, the Soviet choice, in his place. This took place with the presence in the country of Soviet deputy foreign minister Vyshinsky and Soviet troops occupying army headquarters. It was, of course, significant that the great bulk of the Romanian army was out of the country at the time fighting the retreating Germans with the Red Army.

The Romanian government crisis in fact provided a background to the Yalta conference which was being held just along the Black Sea coast. It seriously disturbed the Americans, who refused to recognise the Groza government. The British were reluctant to follow suit as they were more aware of the details of Churchill's prior agreement with Stalin on the country's status. After a meeting of the foreign ministers of the former major Allies in December 1945, some independent ministers were added to the Romanian government. It then secured formal American and British recognition, on the basis that free elections open to all democratic parties would soon be held. Prince Michael was less assured and remained dissatisfied that he had failed to secure the resignation of Groza. By this stage the Prince had retired to the sidelines and was effectively on strike, refusing to sign state documents. It was, in fact, nearly a year before the elections were held, which gave the communists opportunities to harass the independent parties, abolish the senate and introduce various laws establishing new forms of political discrimination and official censorship. The official result of the election, held on 19 November 1946, gave the communist-dominated National Democratic Front 348 parliamentary seats and opposition parties just 35. The remaining independent ministers in the government resigned in protest at the electoral irregularities and opposition deputies refused to take their seats in parliament. The Western governments protested at the violation of the earlier commitment to free elections. But they did not withdraw recognition and signed a peace treaty with Groza's newly strengthened government in February 1947.

Bulgaria

Communist forces launched a rapid and violent drive for power soon after the overthrow of the war-time government. Their campaign stood in marked contrast to the cautious policies masterminded by King Boris until his early death in August 1943. Bulgaria had been forced to allow the Germans rights of passage as well as staging facilities for the invasion of Yugoslavia and Greece. But direct involvement in the hostilities had initially been avoided and the government refused to join the war against the Soviet Union. The inexorable advance of Soviet forces, nevertheless, made Bulgaria's tentative, and relatively undemanding, adherence to the Axis camp increasingly untenable. Romania's change of sides in August 1944 made Bulgarian action imperative. The attitude of its government became increasingly pro-Western and measures were taken to secure an armistice with British and American representatives in Cairo. Rather unwisely no moves were made towards the Soviet Union, with whom Bulgaria had never actually been at war. The Soviet Union declared war on Bulgaria on 5 September 1944 and began to invade three days later, moves that gave it a basis for subsequent action in the country. The same day that the Soviet invasion began Bulgaria declared war on Germany (thus formally bringing it into conflict with all major European Axis and Allied Powers!) and sued for peace with the Russians. The Bulgarian peace initiative was accepted by the Soviet Union and came into effect on 9 September. The same day — and quite possibly without the foreknowledge of the Soviet forces — a 'Fatherland Front', a group claiming to represent national patriotic forces and of which the communists formed a significant part, now seized power.

Bulgaria had maintained a relative detachment from the war, but now entered a period of renewed domestic violence. The Fatherland Front launched a massive wave of executions and reprisals on political rivals. It attacked pro-Westerners and pro-Germans alike in an apparent reassertion of the pattern of political violence that had characterised Bulgarian public life in previous decades. Its effect was to provide the conditions for a rapid and effective seizure of power by the communists. Although Bulgarian communist forces were far weaker than they had been before the war, their political rivals were in no better condition. They offered little resistance to a wholesale purge of the government structure and the subsequent execution of many alleged fascists and war criminals. Some estimates put the number of deaths at 100,000. A communist-inspired reorganisation of the Agrarian Union and Social Democrats were conducted and, by the autumn of 1945, the Fatherland Front had become purely a front for the Communist Party. In November elections were held in which the Front was declared to have won 88 per cent of the vote.

Public distaste for the communist actions was by now considerable and the confidence of the communist forces themselves was getting shaky. Even the Soviet Union had doubts about the domestic position of the communist movement in the country. The communists, nevertheless, continued to move forward. In 1946 the army was purged, Bulgaria declared a republic, the monarch sent into exile and a constituent assembly elected to draft a new constitution. Once the United States ratified the peace treaty with Bulgaria on 4 June 1947 repression intensified. Independent agrarian leader Petkov was arrested on the floor of the parliament the following day and hanged for conspiracy three months later. At the same time, his party was dissolved. Soon after, the remaining social democrat opposition deputies were arrested and sentenced in November 1948 to long prison terms. All opposition to communist rule had now been fully crushed.

Yugoslavia

Conditions in Yugoslavia and Albania were very different from the other countries of the region in that indigenous communist forces played a prominent part in the liberation. German forces had, in any case, been forced to withdraw quickly after the rapid Soviet advance through Romania and Hungary, leaving strongly pro-Soviet groups in power there from the outset. Yugoslav communist leader Tito's authority had risen markedly throughout 1944, not just because of the growing success of his partisan movement against the Germans but also because of his political status within the country as a whole. In May 1944 the exiled King Peter dropped the monarchist resistance leader Mihajlović as his war minister. In September he called for all Yugoslavs to support Tito in his campaign to drive out the German forces. By the middle of October Tito and his partisans were able to occupy Belgrade, the country's capital.

The phoney government coalitions and dubious political fronts seen elsewhere in Eastern Europe were absent in Yugoslavia, where the People's Front described itself straightforwardly as a bloc of communists and non-party sympathisers. It was on this basis that 90.5 per cent of voters endorsed the Front in elections during November 1945 which were probably far more authentic than those held in the other countries. The government also promoted social and economic policies that were far closer to those of the Soviet Union than anywhere else in the region at this stage. This particularly concerned the extensive nationalisation of economic resources and collectivisation of agriculture. The management of the economy as a whole became increasingly centralised. Tito's influence extended to exert a large influence over communist liberation forces in Albania. But it was also in Yugoslavia that the earliest resistance to Soviet power in Eastern Europe was to emerge. This paradoxical development came very quickly, just as the process of imposing Soviet control over the rest of Eastern Europe was being completed. Friction between Soviet representatives and the Yugoslav leadership began to develop at an early stage and an open split occurred in 1948 (of which further details later on pages 103-4), around the same time that the Soviet hold over Czechoslovakia was strengthening.

Czechoslovakia

Churchill drew attention in a speech at Fulton, Missouri, as early as February 1946 to the descent of an Iron Curtain separating Eastern Europe from the West. This notion effectively defined a new Eastern Europe that characterised the post-Second World War period just as the idea of a region of nation-states had reflected the preoccupations of 1919. But the consolidation of communist rule in Czechoslovakia was still two years ahead at the time of Churchill's speech, and it was that development which helped confirm the full development of cold war relations between the two superpowers. Czechoslovakia had been distinguished not just by its relatively well established pluralist tradition but also by strong electoral support for its Communist Party. The Red Army was also absent from the country during the critical period of political transition. Soviet forces withdrew in October 1945 together with those of the United States.

But Soviet pressure and decisive action in pursuit of the goals pursued by Stalin throughout the region were by no means lacking in Czechoslovakia. The Soviet leader, for example, felt no compunction about annexing the far eastern part of the country, Ruthenia (inhabited essentially by Ukrainians), an action similar to that taken against Poland. Zdeněk Fierlinger, a nominal social democrat but known communist sympathiser, was also installed as prime minister until elections were held in 1946. The communists gained 38 per cent of the vote in that ballot, following which their leader Klement Gottwald became prime minister and headed a coalition government. This operated quite smoothly and communist authority was exercised along reasonably constitutional lines until the United States launched the Marshall Plan for European economic recovery the following year.

The changing international environment

The Marshall Plan was a substantial and generously funded programme to support post-war European economic development, and was imaginatively conceived to tackle the dire situation of post-war Europe. Participation was offered by the United States to all European countries — although some have maintained that it was deliberately orientated to promote West European development along capitalist lines, confirming the isolation of the communist Soviet Union and its committed allies. That was certainly the outcome the Plan produced and it played a distinctive part in consolidating monopolistic communist rule in Czechoslovakia. Like Poland, the country's government initially accepted an invitation to participate in a preliminary conference on the Plan but was then required on Soviet orders to reject it. For foreign minister Jan Masaryk, son of Tomáš, the founder of the original Czechoslovak state, it was an ominous indication of how limited the country's freedom of action now was. Under Soviet control and the dictatorship of Stalin's local representatives the states of Eastern Europe were increasingly separated from those of the West. There was an increasingly sharp physical divorce in terms of fortified borders and restrictions on foreign travel. The whole culture of Eastern Europe as well as diverse forms of political, economic and social organisation were developing along different lines from those in the West.

In September 1947 the Cominform, or Communist Information Bureau, was founded as an organisation designed to promote a common path of development within the Soviet zone of influence. At its initial meeting the 'complete victory of the working class over the bourgeoisie in every East European land except Czechoslovakia' was explicitly noted. The observation directed attention to the growing distinctiveness of its relative democracy and independence in a region of intensifying Stalinist control. In response to the expulsion of communists from coalition governments in France and Italy, the Czechoslovak leadership moved to strengthen links between communists and social democrats. The threat of communist groups becoming marginalised there as was increasingly the case in Western Europe was hardly a conceivable one, and the move was clearly designed to strengthen the communist position. A number of domestic crises also increased the political tension in Czechoslovakia. Political confrontation was not regarded with disfavour by the communists as they feared that further elections, due to be held in May 1948, might not see a repetition of the victory they had secured in 1946. They therefore launched a campaign to organise the election on the basis of proportionately organised single-party lists that would simply be presented to the electorate for general approval. This raised considerable fears on the part of the democratic parties.

The Prague *coup*

The 'salami tactics' (by means of which opposition groups were progressively sliced away) as developed in Hungary were also put into operation in Slovakia. Leaders of the Democratic Party were accused of involvement in an anti-state conspiracy and compelled to accept a restructuring of the government in which the communists gained overall control. In Prague it also became evident that the communist minister of the interior was stacking the police force with communist supporters. When he ignored a cabinet decision to halt the process, on 20 February 1948 a number of independent ministers proceeded to resign from the government. The net effect of this move was just to increase communist control in the government. The same day as the resignations, communists formed an armed 15,000-strong people's militia. Armed trade unionists paraded in Prague and the offices of opposition parties were ransacked. Ludvik Svoboda, the head of the army and communist sympathiser, pledged military support for 'the people' without consulting the president. Against a background of diverse forms of extra-parliamentary pressure, mass demonstrations of working-class communists and other signs of a stage-managed revolutionary drama, President Beneš bowed to what now seemed inevitable and sanctioned the formation of a strongly communist-dominated government. He had made little attempt to rally democratic forces or to build on the confrontation that crystallised with the resignation of the non-communist government ministers. Beneš clearly had an over-optimistic view of future developments in the Soviet Union and East European policy.

Churchill's identification of an Iron Curtain, somewhat premature at the time, now looked much more convincing. It still remains a matter of conjecture how far Stalin aimed to dominate post-war Eastern Europe from the outset and to what extent the pattern of strengthening Soviet influence emerged in more piecemeal fashion. Western views of the region had changed as the war progressed. Few clear post-war objectives for the region were, in any case, defined in discussions between the leaders of the war-time alliance. Stalin had plenty of opportunities to build on his basic ambitions. He clearly aimed to secure Soviet interests in Poland and Romania, on which he also had specific territorial designs in which the Western Powers largely acquiesced. But Bulgaria and Hungary also saw the rapid advance of communist forces, a development undoubtedly influenced by the presence of the Red Army. The pattern of growing Soviet influence suggests that legitimate security concerns, wholly understandable in the light of recent German aggression, were taken to extremes of political control where the agencies of military force were also present. The Western Powers had few means of preventing such developments, but showed little major interest in them during the early stages either.

Few efforts were made, for example, to secure the 'free and unfettered elections' called for in the Yalta agreement. Peace treaties were signed by the Western Powers with Romania and Bulgaria and were clearly an issue of importance for communist authorities and the Soviet leadership — despite signs that the incumbent governments were not adhering to previous agreements. This seemed to give their leaders the green light to progress towards full dictatorship. US eagerness to consolidate relations with Western Europe (France and West Germany) and the southern flank (Italy, Greece and Turkey), as well as growing military co-operation with the countries of this area, encouraged the Soviet Union likewise to maximise security in terms of military links and the establishment of strong communist governments elsewhere in Eastern Europe. Communist actions in Eastern Europe went far beyond what seemed to be implied by the establishment of a Soviet zone of influence. By the time of the communist *coup* in Czechoslovakia, communist control on the Soviet model was already generally well-established throughout the regime, with the marked exception of Yugoslavia where the former allies had already fallen out.

The break with Yugoslavia

The origins of the Soviet-Yugoslav split were partly a matter of timing. Tito's war-time successes and relatively strong domestic power base were without parallel anywhere else in Eastern Europe except Albania. This background gave him the confidence and capacity not just to pursue radical communist policies in Yugoslavia itself but also to adopt provocative anti-Western attitudes that Stalin himself regarded as risky and unnecessary during 1945 and 1946. They included the pursuit of territorial claims in the Trieste area and continuing support for communist guerrillas in Greece when Stalin was keen to observe the terms of the agreement with Churchill. Just as unwelcome for Stalin was Tito's triumphalist behaviour on visits to various East European capitals and his tendency to air imaginative views on the future of the Balkans, where his domestic authority and political success lent him the manner of a natural regional leader. Much of the problem lay precisely in the air of confidence and success that flowed naturally from Tito's war-time experience in Yugoslavia. He just had no need to cultivate the relations of subservience and dependence on the Soviet leadership that were unavoidable for communist leaders elsewhere in Eastern Europe.

More concrete issues also entered into the situation. The Soviet military advisers seconded to the Yugoslav forces from 1945 behaved as they did elsewhere in the Soviet zone of influence. They were arrogant and contemptuous of local officials, generally treating them like backward subjects of a greater imperial civilisation. In more practical terms, Stalin caused great resentment by restricting the supply of spare parts for Yugoslavia's armaments in an attempt to limit Tito's freedom of action. Neither were the Soviets impressed by the rapid pace of Yugoslavian industrialisation, and preferred a greater emphasis on agriculture and the exploitation of raw materials. This implied a position of continuing dependence for the Yugoslav economy and the perpetuation of patterns of trade which profited the Soviet Union. The establishment of the joint companies favoured by the Soviet Union was not welcomed by the Yugoslav leadership, and Tito stopped their development after February 1947.

Personality and political attitudes also seemed to play a large part in their own right. Stalin was certainly known for his arrogance and condescension to those regarded as inferior. But part of the problem also lay with Yugoslav insensitivity and the self-regarding nature of their own leaders, as the Yugoslavs did not realise the nature of the effect their behaviour was producing. Understandably, perhaps, they underestimated the degree to which Stalin required subordination in all areas and the growing resentment that continuing signs of independence produced. It fed the paranoia that was soon to give rise in Eastern Europe to the purges and show-trials that had wracked the Soviet Union during the 1930s.

Tensions between Stalin and the Yugoslav leadership came to a head at a meeting in the Kremlin on 10 February 1948. Stalin accused Tito of making plans to set up a Balkan federation behind his back. In March, the Soviet Union recalled its military and civilian advisers and proceeded to accuse the Yugoslav Communist Party of ideological heresy. It claimed that the Yugoslav organisation was undemocratic and extensively infiltrated by British spies. The Yugoslavs took vigorous action to defend themselves, which only inflamed the situation. The Soviet leadership responded with increasingly vicious criticism and on 28 June 1948 expelled them from the Cominform, the international agency set up the preceding year to promote communist integration. The accompanying allegations of conspiracy, treachery, nationalism and ideological deviation then fed directly into the politics of the other East European states. They soon provided a major agency for the intensification of Soviet control throughout the region.

The pattern of regional political development

By this stage, developments after 1945 had provided a clear indication of what the previously agreed 'sphere of Soviet influence' in Eastern Europe actually meant (see page 90). After the crucial conferences held at Yalta and Potsdam communist rule was imposed with increasing firmness. Direct or indirect Soviet pressure played a major part in the process in all countries apart from Yugoslavia and Albania. It involved a reshaping of Eastern Europe in line with Soviet interests that took little account of the states' formal independence or the political preferences of their inhabitants. A general pattern of development that encompassed these changes has been suggested in terms of (1) coalition building and the establishment of formally multi-party governments in which the communists actually exerted as much influence as they could, (2) the application of increasing pressure on democratic and centrist forces to reduce the independence of all organisations and political figures to rule out the possibility of anti-communist opposition, and (3) followed by the total domination of communist groups within their domestic sphere of operation. Hungary followed this model most closely, with Czechoslovakia having a more extended, nearly three-year spell of multi-party government. But Poland,

Romania and Bulgaria did not see such a distinct sequence and failed to go through any real multi-party phase. By 1948 any such sequence of change had run its brief course. All opposition parties were eliminated (although some pro-establishment auxiliary organisations still called parties were allowed to continue in existence), socialist bodies were purged and merged with increasingly dominant communist parties, and Soviet-style one-party rule was replicated throughout the region.

In Poland the critical stage was reached after elections in 1947 when the position of the communists was considerably strengthened and later, in March 1948 just after the *coup* in Czechoslovakia, when it was announced that the Socialist and Communist Parties would merge to form a supposedly United Workers' Party. The position of the Hungarian communists, on the other hand, was still not fully assured after the 1947 elections. Only after then were parties which still had some degree of independence further pressured or dissolved. Socialists who continued to resist were expelled from the party, and the rest merged with the communists to form a new Workers' Party in June 1948. This gave the Hungarian communists complete control of the government.

A similar process occurred in Czechoslovakia after the *coup*. Non-competitive elections — in which voters were simply invited to endorse the candidate put forward — were held after the dissolution of parliament in May 1948 and the Social Democratic Party was merged with the communists during the summer of 1948. The process took its toll in terms of Czechoslovakia's leading democratic political figures. Foreign minister Jan Masaryk died on 10 March after a fall from his office window, the official verdict of suicide still being subject to much doubt and by no means universally accepted. Having sworn in a communist government, too, President Beneš resigned on 6 June and died three months later. Similar pressures were exerted in Romania during 1947, and the King was forced to abdicate on 30 December. In February 1948 what was left of the Romanian Social Democratic Party was merged with the communists. The remaining Bulgarian social democrats were similarly mopped up by the Communist Party in August 1948. The diverse paths of post-war change led inexorably to a uniform pattern of monolithic communist dictatorship.

Stalinist purges and the terror process

The Sovietisation of Eastern Europe was a progressive process. The countries of the region were forced into the Stalinist mould in several distinct phases. The establishment of one-party rule on Soviet lines was a phase that was largely completed by the end of 1948. But this was by no means the end of the process. The imposition of communist dictatorship was accompanied by the increasing prominence of the security forces, the imposition of a police state and growing repression of virtually all independent social forces (including the Church). In the wake of the Soviet-

Yugoslav split this developed into show trials of prominent party figures whose fundamental loyalty to the communist cause and to Stalin himself could not realistically be doubted. The newly installed ruling parties were now purged to ensure even greater compliance with the directives of Stalin and his representatives. Terror was applied to those suspected of harbouring opposition tendencies and to extract confessions from all deviants who failed to follow the official party line. 'Titoism' now became a prominent and apparently widespread heresy throughout the East European parties. The charges of treachery, sabotage and spying most likely had no basis at all. But sympathy for Tito's defence of his nation's interests and his capacity to criticise some aspects of Soviet policy was more widespread.

'Native' communists who had spent the war underground in their own country rather than in exile and under the close scrutiny of Soviet agents in Moscow were particularly suspect. Polish leader, Władysław Gomułka, refused to renounce his belief in a 'Polish road to socialism', which included avoiding the horrors and economic devastation associated with the collectivisation of peasant agriculture as practised in the Soviet Union. He opposed the establishment of the Cominform and reaffirmed his political views in June 1948, behaviour which led to his replacement as party leader in September on grounds of national deviation, distortion of the role of the party and undermining the class struggle in the countryside. But only in November 1949 was he removed from the party's Central Committee and even then he stayed in government employment for some time.

Others suffered a more cruel fate. The communist takeover of Hungary had been more rapid than that of Poland, but the violence and intensity of dictatorship during the period of full Stalinism was more pronounced. In May 1949 László Rajk, another 'native' communist, Hungarian foreign minister and previously head of that country's ministry of the interior, was arrested and charged with espionage as well as nationalist deviation. After torture he confessed to a variety of wholly unbelievable crimes and admitted to having been an agent of imperialism as far back as the Spanish Civil War. Like other communist leaders, he was now seen as being part of an extensive imperialist conspiracy in which Tito played a key role. On 15 October 1949 Rajk was executed with other former party leaders. This prompted charges from the British and US governments that Hungary was committing human rights abuses and acting in breach of the peace treaty. In Bulgaria party leader, Traicho Kostov, was himself involved. Like others at the time he had been active in the domestic underground, and was deformed by injuries suffered in a jail escape during an earlier period. After the war he was vociferous in defending Bulgarian interests against Soviet economic exploitation. Under the current conditions in Eastern Europe this was guilt enough, and he was hanged in December 1949.

Document: Accusations made against László Rajk, September 1949.

The American and British intelligence services purchased Tito and his clique even during the war against Hitler, to prevent the national and social liberation of the peoples of south-eastern Europe, to isolate the Soviet Union, and to prepare the third world war. The anti-Soviet plan for the Balkan bloc was born not in Tito's head but in the intelligence offices of Washington and London. The *putsch* in Hungary, planned by Tito and his clique to be put into action by Rajk's spy ring, cannot be understood out of the context of the international plans of the American imperialists. Let us remember what Rajk said about the timing of the armed *putsch*. By this he meant the selection of a favourable moment from the point of view of world politics, that is, of a moment when the Soviet Union would be tied down, in order to allow free hands for the Yugoslav adventurers to carry out their internal and external armed intervention against the Hungarian People's Republic.

As time passed and the Stalinist system became more entrenched the purges became yet more extensive. A major investigation in Czechoslovakia during early 1950 focused mostly on officials responsible for foreign policy and trade. It had a particular feature in that many arrested were Jewish and were charged, amongst other things, with having subversive links with the recently established Israeli state. Foreign minister Clementis was soon himself caught up in the process. In November 1951 former party chief Slánský, known for his own ruthlessness and the vicious application of terror, was also arrested. After a trial the following year 11 of the accused were hanged. Following further proceedings, 50 of the 97 party Central Committees were removed and six of the seven Central committee secretaries eliminated. The scope of the purge widened to include large segments of Czech and Slovak society. Ordinary party members were affected throughout Eastern Europe and around a quarter of all party members in the region were ejected from communist organisations, over half a million being removed in Czechoslovakia alone. But the process could be turned to political advantage by some individuals. In Romania Gheorghiu-Dej was able to strengthen his position in 1952 by forging a new alliance against 'Muscovite' leaders, Luca and Pauker, and taking over the premiership from Petru Groza, by these means succeeding in dominating Romanian politics until his death in 1965.

Economic and social transformation

The changes that the extension of Soviet influence brought were not only political. Stalin's victory over Eastern Europe and the imposition of the Stalinist system throughout the region meant a number of things. In political terms it meant: the strengthening and more direct exercise of Soviet power throughout the Iron Curtain countries (although Stalin proved unable and ultimately unwilling to bring Yugoslavia back into the fold); growing uniformity and social regimentation; stronger central control over political and social organisations; and greater repression and intimidation of the countries' inhabitants. But it also had a strong economic component in terms of centralised patterns of industrial development and the collectivisation of agriculture. A Committee for Mutual Economic Assistance (COMECON) was established in 1949, but showed few signs of activity in its early years and had only limited success in achieving real economic integration. On the other hand, the rise of a unified party-state and imposition of monopolistic political rule was accompanied by policies of comprehensive economic development and industrialisation that were by no means inappropriate to the long-standing economic problems of much of Eastern Europe.

Rapid industrialisation seemed to offer an effective solution to the massive over-population of much of the East European countryside and the persistent problems of rural poverty (see pages 44-5). Free markets had not provided a solution between the wars and a centralised system of state management presented a promising alternative. The nationalisation of trade and industry gathered pace in 1948, and by the end of the year embraced 80 per cent of the economy in the more developed countries of Czechoslovakia, Hungary and Poland (see Table below). By 1950 the application of central planning in both industry and agriculture meant that at least half the East European countries' material product was generated by the socialist sector. Initially, at least, attention was paid to domestic conditions and governments retained some capacity to pursue national paths of economic development. But principles of relatively sound planning soon escalated into the imposition of wholly unrealistic investment and production targets. The plans developed and followed in 1948-49 differed considerably from amended versions developed in 1950-51.

Indices of socialisation, 1952		
	Share of socialised sector %	Socialisation of the agricultural area %
	Industry Trade	
Albania	98 88	6
Bulgaria	100 98	61
Czechoslovakia	98 97	43
Hungary	97 82	37
Poland	99 93	17
Romania	97 76	25

The original plans represented ambitious and highly demanding projects for industrial growth, but they did not threaten the degree of economic imbalance or reflect the disregard for the living standards of the population that became evident in the final variant. From already low levels, real wages fell by 15 per cent between 1950 and 1953 in Hungary, 8 per cent in Poland and 5 per cent in Czechoslovakia. This was largely the consequence of excessive levels of investment in heavy industry and the military sector. In Hungary, for example, the final plan targets provided for a massive 60 per cent increase in investment levels for heavy industry over the 1950-54 period, around 50 per cent in Czechoslovakia and a similar level in Poland. This meant that agriculture, light and consumer industries, the service sector and housing could not fail to be affected, and living standards — which in many cases had only made a partial recovery from war-time devastation — were badly hit. In agriculture, too, the early phase of policy built on sound measures of land reform adopted in the immediate post-war years. But the relatively moderate collectivisation programme of 1948 was followed by a more extreme variant in the early 1950s. It was, in this as in other areas, really after 1949 that Stalinism came into full prominence and reached its ultimate level of development. The international environment again played a major part here, and the intensification of the cold war between the West and the communist camp had a direct influence on economic planning, particularly after the outbreak of the Korean War on 25 June 1950, which placed the East European economies on a major war footing.

The effects of the industrialisation drive

The socialist industrialisation drive of the late 1940s and the overall programme of economic development associated with it certainly produced high official rates of growth in the early stages. This followed directly from enormously high levels of investment devoted to heavy industry which, for the most part, did little to improve the living standards or material situation of much of the population. But actual growth rates, it later emerged, were nothing like as high as those claimed at the time by the East European governments. Growth was, too, more rapid in the less developed countries where high levels of early industrial growth had an immediate economic effect. Such is generally the case when substantial portions of the rural population move into towns and take up industrial employment (as also happened in post-war France during the immediate post-war years).

But the rate of growth was less impressive in a country like Czechoslovakia, where industrial development was already well advanced and war-time destruction minimal. The major economic problem here was the acute shortage of labour and there was a shortfall of around 200,000 workers in 1945, a factor closely related to the expulsion of the German population from post-war Czechoslovakia. Underlying this situation was the radical turn towards a war economy in all countries of the Soviet bloc, which came on top of an initial hike of capital investment levels by the new communist governments 30-40 per cent above those applied in the immediate post-war reconstruction period. Ambitious growth targets were further stretched to favour the output of more producer goods with correspondingly less provision for agriculture, housing and light industry. Much of the production this generated went straight to the Soviet Union and supported the war effort. Stalin was also determined to extract compensation for the massive Soviet losses incurred during the war. It took economic reparations from the defeated powers but also imposed punishing terms of trade on its new East European partners which brought them major losses. At precisely this time the United States was contributing substantial resources to the economic reconstruction of Western Europe under the provisions of the Marshall Plan. Subsequent estimates showed that the Soviet Union had extracted just about the same amount from Eastern Europe as the United States was pumping into the West of the Continent (calculated variously at from $14 to 20 billion).

The social consequences of communist rule

The overwhelming emphasis on heavy industry and military productions, accompanied by a general bias towards Soviet interests, had a direct effect on wage levels and the living standards of the working population. While much was heard of the proletarian basis of communist rule and a form of government oriented to working-class interests, this was certainly not apparent in direct material terms. Wage levels fell throughout the region. In the absence of authentic trade unions or independent political parties the population had little means of redress, or even ways to express their dissatisfaction or opposition to developments under communist rule. But there were certainly local outbursts of frustration which were severely dealt with. The strong flow of capital investment meant that funds for agriculture, consumer goods and housing were all cut. As real wages fell, inflation levels rose — largely as a result of the growth in employment and failure of supplies of consumer goods to keep pace. Consumer prices rose by 80 per cent in Poland between 1950 and 1953, and by 70 per cent in Hungary. Rationing was reintroduced in most countries, and was kept in Hungary, Czechoslovakia and Poland until 1953. To restore some kind of equilibrium monetary reform was introduced (during 1950 in Poland and 1953 in Czechoslovakia), which had the further effect of reducing public purchasing power and cutting the value of people's savings. The East European economies were, therefore, subject to major imbalances. Yet not all was bad news.

The picture was considerably less bleak if the more general social context was taken into account. A major emphasis in government policy was placed on both general and vocational education, new opportunities became available for underprivileged groups and paths of social mobility were opened up. The market for farm produce was strong and agricultural underemployment — the great economic curse of the inter-war period — declined. Large numbers migrated from rural areas to the towns. Off-farm employment rose by 34 per cent in Poland between 1950 and 1955, by 20 per cent in Hungary and even by 15 per cent in Czechoslovakia. Mobility was social in nature as well as geographical. Manual workers were promoted to foremen and advanced managerial positions. The needs of extensive industrial construction and high demand for building workers helped improve the earning capacity of manual workers and reduced wage inequality. An increasing proportion of women were able to find employment outside the agricultural sector and undertook work in industry (although this tendency was limited in Poland where small-scale peasant agriculture was hung on to more tenaciously and the labour demands of farm work remained strong).

The Stalinist model of economic development was, therefore, not without its virtues in Eastern Europe. In particular, the early measures of post-war land reform, although soon followed by less popular policies of collectivisation, helped counter the over-population that had been such a persistent problem not just in countries like Romania, but also in more developed areas like Hungary and Poland. Even more significant for this process was the rapid development of heavy industry. This helped provide demand for the pool of under-used labour as well as the produce of the agricultural sector. Such consequences of economic planning and state-sponsored social engineering proved highly attractive to some sectors of the population after the Depression and the dire effects it had produced throughout the 1930s. With the failure of democracy in much of the region in the inter-war period, followed by the nightmare of a further war and Nazi occupation, there was support in many quarters for the radically different solution that Soviet communism seemed to offer.

But there was an enormous political downside. Whatever attractions the communist model might have had, they did not last long for much of the population in view of the tyrannical nature of the dictatorship that accompanied it. The advantages of socialist industrialisation, too, petered out at an early stage and left the eastern countries at a considerable disadvantage to those that had taken the western path of development. Although Stalin died on 5 March 1953 his legacy, whilst amended and partially reformed, lasted for several more decades and it was not until 1989 that Eastern Europe was finally able to break out of the straitjacket that Stalin had imposed on it.

Questions to consider

- What view did the Soviet leadership take of Eastern Europe in 1945?
- How and why was the Eastern Europe of 1945 different from that of 1918?
- What did its location in the Soviet sphere of influence mean for Eastern Europe?
- What was Stalinism and what effects did it have?
- What links can be drawn between the political and economic aspects of change?

● The social consequences of communist rule

7 Histories of Eastern Europe

Interpretations and historical accounts of the past often depend very much on who is making them and when they are made. With regard to Eastern Europe between 1918 and 1953, it is very much the when that counts at the current time. The end of communist rule in Eastern Europe in 1989, or at least its radical transformation, has cast a strong new light on its history during the earlier part of the century. This particularly concerns the status of communism and the permanence of its place, however controversial, in the developing programme of human civilisation which many people have claimed to be able to identify. Whatever its shortcomings, however unpleasant the experience of living in the shadow of Soviet power and however unattractive and inefficient the political and economic system that prevailed in the countries affected, before 1989 it seemed that communist Eastern Europe was there to stay. None seriously foresaw its demise, and ruling groups in Hungary, Poland and the Soviet Union who busied themselves with questions and processes of reform during 1988 and early 1989 thought they were reforming the communist system, not destroying it. Whatever the nature of communist Eastern Europe, most agreed that it was permanent and not at all likely to disappear in the foreseeable future. All this changed in 1989 with the sequence of developments that began (at least in a public sense) with the Polish elections in June of that year.

In the case of the communist period it was, indeed, essentially its status as the basis for Eastern Europe's future that was subject to reappraisal. Historians in Eastern Europe itself now have incomparably greater freedom to write full histories of the region and particular aspects of its development, and much better materials on which to base their analyses. But the view taken of the communist past, and particularly its Stalinist origins, has hardly been changed in any radical sense. Stalinism and its effects had few defenders either in the East or the West, and recent history has been distinguished by its depth and use of newly available sources rather than by any new approach or novel interpretation. The range of historical interpretation has, to some extent, been narrowed by the disappearance of official spokesmen for the later incarnation of the communist regime who felt that its Stalinist origins should not be disparaged in quite such strong terms as those used by many western historians and informal domestic critics. But even such relative apologists just tended to gloss over the crimes and mistakes of the Stalinist period rather than attempt to justify them in any form of historical analysis. To this extent, it is less the nature of the analysis that has changed than its depth and quality.

Historical views of the inter-war period have also changed. But, again, it is not so much the interpretation that has been transformed as the relevance and immediacy of the pre-communist and the pre-war period that has suddenly been enhanced. The past has been shunted forward into the present. Eastern Europe's inter-war years have suddenly become a part of modern history in a way that was inconceivable before 1989. As one contributor to a symposium on the implications of 1989 in the American inter-disciplinary journal *East European Politics and Societies* put it, study of the region's recent history must now begin not in 1945 but in 1918. This does not refer just to the general framework of academic study, either.

Topics that had once been laid to rest within the safe historical confines of the inter-war period have returned to the contemporary agenda. Radical anti-communism, anti-Semitism and nationalism emerge once more as major contemporary issues and their significance is debated within the context of a new democracy. Democracy and economic backwardness — as ever, a relative concept — is again a primary concern of East European leaders and Western policy-makers in a new global context. It is, of course, one quite unforeseen by the architects of social industrialisation and the communist road to modernity in the late 1940s, and raises the old question of East European backwardness to a new level. There is also a new German question, as the small and medium-sized countries of Eastern Europe struggle to develop mutually secure and profitable relations with their immediate western neighbour. Neither does the exclusion of Russia from much of its sphere of post-war influence remove all tensions or uncertainties from Eastern Europe's other frontier. All three topics that have provided the themes for the main chapters of this book thus re-emerge in recognisable form in contemporary Eastern Europe.

In terms of historical analysis and the interpretation of topics related to the major German and Russian themes that have critically affected the course of East European development, the main thrust of discussion continues to be conducted between historians whose major interests lie outside the East European area itself. While their views have great significance for the topics studied here, the main dynamics of the situations they have examined operate in a different context. The importance of the rise of Nazism and expansion of German power during the 1930s can hardly be exaggerated. But it is historians of Germany who debate over the origins of the process and argue about the particular part played by Hitler and his small group of extremists in distinction to the influence of a particular path of state development and the impact of an authoritarian political culture. Equally, the sources of Soviet expansionism and the emergence of the cold war have been debated by Soviet historians and experts in international relations, respectively, rather than by historians of Eastern Europe, even if they are developments that have had a profound influence on the pattern of East European history.

If the question of the independence of the East European states was largely pre-empted by the nature of developments in Germany and Russia, as well as by broader features of international relations, issues of internal politics and the fate of their democratic order during the inter-war period have often been understood as the outcome of domestic factors. The introduction to *The Columbia History of Eastern Europe in the Twentieth Century* (1992) thus attributed the general failure of the democratic experiment in Eastern Europe during the inter-war period primarily to internal forces. But it is not an opinion that all have shared. Its adequacy has been briefly examined towards the end of Chapter 4 of this book (pages 53-5) and was also discussed in a critical light in an extended review in *Contemporary European History* (1994). It was indeed true that most new East European democracies failed in the 1920s, before the more obvious international disasters of the Depression and the Nazi ascendancy struck. But the formation of the new states and the conditions of their democratic development were determined by the views of the victorious powers and were very much the product of the international framework in place at the close of the First World War.

It is notable that this judgement on the nature of developments in the newly established Eastern Europe of the 1920s was both historical and one linked firmly with contemporary concerns. The need to re-evaluate the region's history and draw conclusions that had some relevance to the sudden appearance of a post-communist Eastern Europe was strongly felt. The creation after the First World War of a modern Eastern Europe on principles of national democracy was an attractive point of reference. One of the characteristics of East European histories and, indeed, of the region as a whole has been that of repeated renewal and a susceptibility to radical reinterpretation. If the eighteenth century invented an Eastern Europe of backwardness and comparative savagery (see pages 11-13), the early twentieth century saw one of national democracy and the restoration of identity (page 28). A darker picture, nevertheless, soon obscured the early hopes. The end of communist Eastern Europe brought questions of democracy and independence into prominence once more.

One of the other main problems identified in the recent review in *Contemporary European History* was less the adequacy of one particular interpretation of modern East European history than the general absence of recent accounts and of a synthesised study of the region in the twentieth century as a whole from a contemporary standpoint. Few have sought to outline or explain the history of modern Eastern Europe as a whole. It has remained something of a sphere apart, scrutinised on occasion by those with related but distinctive interests in other historical areas, or analysed in separate portions by those with an interest in one of its numerous countries. This book is, indeed, one of relatively few in recent years to provide an overview of the region as a whole. More new histories which trace its developments will doubtless emerge as the outside world finds its attention more closely drawn once more to Eastern Europe and its unique problems and possibilities.

8 Eastern Europe Continuity and Change

The Eastern Europe that had emerged in 1953 was a very different one from that seen in 1918. It was, to start from basics, located in a slightly different area. To the extent that major regions can be said to move, 'Eastern Europe' had in some places shifted 50 miles or more to the West. What was generally called Eastern Europe in 1953 were the countries that lay between West Germany (the Federal Republic) and the Soviet Union (it also included East Germany, but this turned out to be a temporary addition). Post-war Poland now included substantial areas of former German territory, while East Prussia and the problematic Polish Corridor (see page 65) had disappeared. In similar fashion, the Soviet Union included parts of former Poland, as well as smaller portions of Czechoslovakia and Romania, and had reabsorbed the Baltic states. The Eastern Europe of 1953 was a smaller and strictly communist one. No one now thought of Greece or (perhaps with less confidence) Austria as part of the region. Any hopes of the development of the post-war East European states as parliamentary democracies had now disappeared, as had most ambitions of national independence in the foreseeable future. All expectation in this area had not been extinguished, it is true, although virtually all that remained was snuffed out in 1956 with the repression of the Hungarian Revolution.

But major social and economic changes were under way. An enormous programme of industrialisation had been launched, small peasant holdings were being merged into collective farms, and the impoverished pool of unemployed labour that had marked the depressed 1930s was rapidly being drained. The Eastern Europe of 1953 seemed, in economic as well as other terms, a very different one from that of 1918. Elements of continuity and change in twentieth-century East European history have, nevertheless, been closely interwoven. Those of continuity continued to make their presence felt, and actually appeared stronger in 1989 than they did in 1953. The communist model of economic development turned out to carry its own problems of flexibility, pollution and capacity to satisfy consumer needs, even if it took several decades and repeated attempts at partial reform for it to run out of steam completely. When its failure was recognised in 1989, certain elements of continuity with inter-war Eastern Europe suddenly came into prominence. Massive economic changes had been occurring outside the communist camp, particularly in association with developments in information technology, and the region once more came to be one of economic backwardness. As the dinosaur industries that had occupied pride of place in the socialist industrialisation drive were exposed to the new economic climate, large numbers of workers came on to the labour market and unemployment once more surfaced as a serious social and economic problem.

Neither had the sources of former political tension dried up. Nationalism and virulent ethnic prejudice, once thought to have been discredited by the rise and actions of the Nazis throughout Europe and superseded by the internationalist outlook and ideology of the socialist movement, also reappeared as a significant force. Its consequences were most violent and destructive in the former Yugoslavia, but they also found some part to play in the political processes of most East European countries in the 1990s.

The end of communism also meant the rebirth of liberal democracy. The main question in this context was whether the conditions that prevailed at the end of the twentieth century were more conducive to its development and consolidation than they had been at the beginning. Such starting-points had been seen before. As well as 1989, 1918 and 1945 were both dates that seemed to promise a hopeful future for a new Eastern Europe. They led, either directly or more slowly, to major disappointment in terms of loss of national independence and most civic freedoms — but also to the eventual defeat of the repressive powers. Other dates, like 1939 and 1948, were more symbolic of Eastern Europe's descent into dictatorship. In terms of the final date of this history, too, the dictatorship in place in 1953 was for many inhabitants of the region strongly reminiscent of the situation under the Nazis just ten years before. But it, too, was not to last. 1989, with the final exhaustion of the long-lasting Soviet domination, seemed therefore to reach back to the radical new beginning of 1918.

The Eastern Europe of the late twentieth century is indeed more similar to the new Eastern Europe of the immediate post-First World War period than to the region newly liberated from the Nazis in 1945. It is more like it in terms of territory, and includes as independent members the Baltic states. Liberation has been based on fundamental changes in the strategic position of the two major powers of the region. Russia is again weakened and able to exert only limited influence over the region. The nature of its future is not clear and the pattern of future relations with the countries of Eastern Europe remains uncertain. Germany, though still smaller than it was even in 1918, is by no means enfeebled in terms of overall power but has now eschewed nationalist ambitions in favour of developing a stronger identity within a broader European framework. Here there is an important change underlying the continuity which has major implications for the place of the eastern countries in Europe as a whole. Lessons seem to have been learnt from the crisis and catastrophe of the 1930s, and in this respect the continuities of East European history now show more promise.

Further Reading

1. General textbooks

No texts cover precisely the 35 turbulent years examined in this book, nor is the geographical coverage quite the same in any of the relevant histories. A particularly lively and full survey of the region as a whole which begins in 1815 is provided by Alan Palmer in *The Lands Between: a History of East-Central Europe since the Congress of Vienna* (1970). Robin Okey's *Eastern Europe, 1740-1980: Feudalism to Communism* (second edition, 1986) is also an excellent introduction. A more narrowly defined east-central Europe is covered over a longer time-span by Piotr S. Wandycz in *The Price of Freedom: a History of East Central Europe from the Middle Ages to the Present* (1992). P. Longworth, *The Making of Eastern Europe* (1992) also takes a broad historical view.

More modern coverage is provided by R.J. Crampton in *Eastern Europe in the Twentieth Century* (second edition 1997), J. Held (ed.), *The Columbia History of Eastern Europe in the Twentieth Century* (1992) and S. Berglund and F. Aarebrot, *The Political History of Eastern Europe in the 20th Century* (1997). Z.A.B. Zeman's perspective in *The Making and Breaking of Communist Europe* (1991) is broader than its title might suggest, and is particularly strong on nationalism and ethnic relations.

One critical aspect of the region's development is examined in detail and expertly discussed in M.C. Kaser (ed.), *The Economic History of Eastern Europe: 1919-1975* (several volumes from 1985).

2. Eastern Europe between the wars

J. Rothschild's *East Central Europe between the Two World Wars* (1974) offers a classic study of the period. Shorter and very useful is *The Little Dictators: the History of Eastern Europe since 1918* (1975) by A. Polonsky, which is really an inter-war history, too, despite its title. Much closer to the period, but very dated for the contemporary reader, is H. Seton Watson's *Eastern Europe between the Wars, 1918-1941* (1946). A further major work in this area is C.A. Macartney and A.W. Palmer, *Independent Eastern Europe* (1966).

3. The communist period

While the period covered is much longer than the Stalin years with which this book is concerned, relevant material will be found in L.P. Morris, *Eastern*

Europe since 1945 (1984), G. and N. Swain, *Eastern Europe since 1945* (1993) and, for a smaller group of countries, the present writer's *Central Europe since 1945* (1994). J. Rothschild's *Return to Diversity: a Political History of East Central Europe since World War II* (second edition, 1994) is an excellent complement to the same author's classic history of the inter-war period.

Index

Index